ILK

D1420758

MEMORIES OF MARYHILL

Also available in this series:

Fred Archer	THE CUCKOO PEN
	THE DISTANT SCENE
	THE VILLAGE DOCTOR
William Cooper	FROM EARLY LIFE
Kathleen Dayus	ALL MY DAYS
	THE BEST OF TIMES
	HER PEOPLE
Denis Farrier	COUNTRY VET
Winifred Foley	NO PIPE DREAMS FOR FATHER
	BACK TO THE FOREST
Peggy Grayson	BUTTERCUP JILL
Jack Hargreaves	THE OLD COUNTRY
Mollie Harris	A KIND OF MAGIC
Angela Hewins	THE DILLEN
Elspeth Huxley	GALLIPOT EYES
Joan Mant	ALL MUCK, NO MEDALS
Brian P. Martin	TALES OF TIME AND TIDE
	TALES OF THE OLD COUNTRYMEN
Victoria Massey	ONE CHILD'S WAR
Phyllis Nicholson	COUNTRY BOUQUET
Gilda O'Neill	PULL NO MORE BINES
Valerie Porter	TALES OF THE OLD COUNTRY VETS
	TALES OF THE OLD WOODLANDERS
Sheila Stewart	LIFTING THE LATCH
Jean Stone	
and Louise Brodie	TALES OF THE OLD GARDENERS
Edward Storey	FEN BOY FIRST
	IN FEN COUNTRY HEAVEN
Nancy Thompson	AT THEIR DEPARTING
Marrie Walsh	AN IRISH COUNTRY CHILDHOOD

Memories of Maryhill

Roderick Wilkinson

ISIS
LARGE PRINT
Oxford, England

First published in Great Britain 1993
by Canongate Academic

Published in Large Print 1997 by ISIS Publishing Ltd,
7 Centremead, Osney Mead, Oxford OX2 0ES,
by arrangement with Roderick Wilkinson

British Library Cataloguing in Publication Data
Wilkinson, Roderick
  Memories of Maryhill. – Large print ed. – (Reminiscence
Series)
  1. Wilkinson, Roderick 2. Large type books 3. Glasgow
(Scotland) – Social conditions 4. Great Britain – History –
20th century
  I. Title
  941.4'43'082'092

ISBN 0-7531-5031-X

Printed and bound by Hartnolls Ltd, Bodmin, Cornwall

To our daughter Sheila who inspired
me to complete these memoirs and
offer them for publication

CONTENTS

CHAPTER
ONE

Braeside Street

There was once a television documentary about the birth of birds. I forget what kind of birds they were — ducks, probably — but the point the narrator was making was that these birds would be affected for life by the first thing they saw as they came out of their shell. And he went on to show that a bird doesn't know or care *who* is its mother: it simply gets a fix on whoever feeds it — and that's that. Interesting.

I didn't know till a few years ago that the day I was born my Aunt Kate delivered me in a single-room house in Braeside Street.

This is not to say that if a kindly old doctor had delivered me, things might have been different. All I *am* saying is that if there's any truth in this "bird" theory applying to human beings and if my Aunt Kate had been a midwife tending hundreds of women giving birth, the city of Glasgow might have a few hundreds more misfits than it has now. I'll say no more than that.

My father, they tell me, was on a train from Rosyth Dockyard because it was March 1917 and he was a shipwright and doubtless got a few days' leave from the war effort to come home and cope with the situation.

Let me tell you about Braeside Street. It's still there

— quite a small street with a hill running from Maryhill Road over past Dunard Street School then down to the better houses with weedy little gardens around Lyndhurst Crescent. The street has tenements on either side. There are about twenty "closes", each leading to twelve houses, three to a storey.

The trouble about writing about a place like Braeside Street is that it was — and still is — very respectable. Poor but very respectable. Stories about working-class life in Glasgow seem never to be complete without the Gorbals or Bridgeton or the wild East End. Glasgow and working-class respectability aren't usually thought to go together for really interesting stories. That is probably why many writers from industrial cities have inverted snobbery.

But the truth about Braeside Street was that the people who lived there when I was a child wore Sunday Best, had regular jobs (if they could get them), buried their dead quietly, had church weddings, went to Aunty Ruby in Rothesay for summer holidays. The men drove trains, delivered mail, inspected water drains, mended windows, forged metal or owned little shops for a living. The women cooked tripe, did the washing on Mondays, bore three children and put down their names with the City Corporation for a house in one of the new Intermediate Schemes that were sprouting in places like Ruchill over beyond the canal or that Land of Hope and Glory with gardens and wide roads, Knightswood.

Looking back, I can't see how places like Braeside Street *could* have been anything else but respectable. Little else was worthwhile in our district. We were miles away from the gangs of London Road, securely elevated above the drunken squalor of the Gallowgate on Saturdays, hopelessly isolated from the struggling Jewish people in Oxford Street.

This was the bleak North side of the city — cold, desolate, windy and no slums to call its own except the nearby Garscube Road and Cowcaddens, where bloated fat women with babies in shawls stood around the pubs on Fridays waiting on their men staggering out. Without the Gaspipe — that's what we called the Garscube Road — people like us might have been insulated all our lives from what we now call slums.

I used to hate Glasgow until I had a good look at other cities in the world. I don't mean New York or Paris or London. I mean the Other cities — the big, sprawling places that have ordinary people in them who are never parodied by actors or comedians or set to music, the cities with no silhouette like Wall Street or the Eiffel Tower or Big Ben.

I always hated saying that I came from Glasgow because it is not very beautiful, it's usually raining and it's not very Scottish. Then I found out when I was in Hamburg that many people there didn't particularly like Germany (I believe Adolph Hitler never visited the city), that Grenoble is a city that could as easily be in Switzerland or Spain as in France, and that that vast area between Sweden and Finland up-country is littered with dreary towns and cities that have dark winter nine months of the year and nobody's ever heard of them. The world seems to be full of unglamorous industrial cities that just happened to grow to that size because there was a

3

succession of booms in textiles or steel or papermaking or — like Venice — gondolas and doges.

Now I've come to realise that being born and growing up in Glasgow is about as distinguished a beginning as in Springfield, Illinois or Toulouse. And it certainly seems to be a luckier lot than a beginning in Poona, India or Nome, Alaska.

It would be foolish, however, to try to pretend that one faceless city is the same as another or that if you've seen one you've seen them all. Although there is nothing very edifying today to see in the miles of unused docks and huge silent cranes and idle shipyards down each bank of the Clyde, we *are* faced with the inevitable fact that Glasgow *did* make the River Clyde and the Clyde did indeed make Glasgow. Unlike other thriving cities near the sea like Bilbao and Liverpool and Aberdeen, Glasgow was nothing — just a clapped-out relic of earlier industries — until the city's leaders put their heads together, raised enormous capital funds and virtually hacked, tore, gouged, deepened and widened that shallow, sluggish river right up from the sea for forty miles in order to establish the mightiest shipbuilding industry in the world. The whole operation took about ten years and at the end of it all Glasgow built more vessels for the world than any other city on the face of it.

I grew up in the years after the Great War. All I knew about this war thing was Uncle Roddy who had been killed in it. My mother talked about him for sixty years. He was her only and younger brother and an obsession.

The years that *I* considered normal, usual, were the

ones we now talk of as The Great Slump. Frankly I don't remember *anything* slumping — least of all me. I ate, slept, went to school, played with other children on the street and frankly didn't think it the least bit peculiar that my father was more often sitting at our kitchen window than out at a shipyard. I never missed a meal, went without clothes, missed a haircut or had a cheerless Christmas all my young life. I looked at a photograph of my class at Dunard Street School the other day and my little jersey and shorts and face looked much the same as the others whose fathers were "constant" in their work.

Dad's unemployment in our house was *part* of us. There was nothing wrong with him except that he was a loser. He never drank a drop. He was civil, intelligent, well-meaning, decent and ineffective. He was also a Communist although he never attended a meeting, raised his voice or wrote a letter to any newspaper in all his life. He was simply an unemployed thinker. And we loved him.

The fact that when he *was* working Dad was a very good shipwright was incidental. In the early 'twenties you could be a very good anything and be out of work. Somehow and sadly, however, among all our male relatives — Uncle Jim in Coatbridge, old Uncle Jock in Nansen Street, old Gaelic Uncle Angus in Kelvinside Avenue, Uncle Ben the telephone linesman — my father always was Poor Wull, the mild-eyed, quiet, inoffensive little man who was unemployed two years out of three. Frankly, I often feel that the year he was *in* work was the oddity; the other two were peaceful and idle.

One of the most unpopular things anybody can say of these contentious, rabble-rousing days is that poor people are not usually miserable people. Only a few of us can say it without being hauled to the gallows or garrotted in public. The very idea that poverty can be related to happiness is enough to send most politicians, newspaper editors and do-gooders into tantrums of hysterical indignation.

The few of us who *can* suggest such an idea have usually been very poor. We've "been there".

What I *do* agree is that unemployment makes people miserable. In fact, from my observation, it eventually destroys them. It's not the scarcity of money or clothes or food or other material things that withers the human being, greys his hair, ages his face to a thousand wrinkles of obsessed worry. It's the losing of his self-respect, the simple fact that what he can do with his hands and brains is not wanted by the rest of us.

There's a relation here with the number of people who retire after a regular hardworking life then die two years later. Insurance companies survive and prosper on this simple actuarial fact.

For this reason, I do not believe that any government in a Western country really knows how to solve the unemployment problem simply because they keep trying to solve it in terms of money. Paying people more to be idle is no answer — *that's* not where the pain is.

Unemployment is a pernicious, creeping, invidious, deadly disease that takes slightly different forms with different people but generally runs in four stages. The first stage is shock, then comes the brave attempt to fight it (out every morning round the factory and yard gates), then the lethargy and finally the dull, stupefied wait for psychological death. Muscles atrophy, senses dull, time-wasting becomes habitual, idle talk and gossip become important, talk *about* work in the past tense is the daily boast.

I have no idea why or how we began life in Braeside Street except that you can be sure my father didn't choose it. He was one of a family of seven who were raised in a two-room-and-kitchen house in Burnside Buildings off Corn Street which was off Cowcaddens. It was off everything — a dirty, small cobblestoned alley directly opposite a small iron foundry, and it smelled. I suppose it was my mother who found the house in Braeside Street and my father decided to sink his principles and join the "gentry".

My mother was of West Highland stock. She was the result of one of the thousands of couples who migrated from the Hebridean islands in the North in the late 'eighties to join the frantic industrial boom around Glasgow. She had two sisters and a brother who, as I say, died in the war.

It should say enough for survival that neither my maternal grandfather nor grandmother could speak a word of English when they came to Glasgow. That was the least of their handicaps. Whisky and ignorance took care of the rest. My grandmother died exhausted but tight-lipped and tight-haired in her 'forties. The family drifted apart, and years later my mother picked up my grandfather from a Church Mission Home at the Round Toll when I was just six or so. I know — I was there when we fetched him to stay with us in our room-and-kitchen house at Number 72 where we had moved that year. His days as a foreman boilermaker were over.

To get back to my mother — she was almost all emotion, reaction, instinctive, vigorous, directionless and utterly devoted to my father, the home and me. She left school in Clydebank at thirteen to work as a labouring girl in Singer's factory. Then she became a seamstress in a small back-street tailors where she met Sadie Kerr who had a brother Jimmy who had a pal called Willie Wilkinson. And that was that. I believe my mother was mainly attracted to him because he didn't drink.

The earliest memories I have of my childhood in that little street in Maryhill are full of love and no money and disorganisation. My mother had been barely educated; to the end of her days writing was a great effort. She said more with her bright Highland eyes than with tongue or pen.

Knowing what I know now, it was she who surely held the three of us together through those years of Means Tests and Aunt Kate's tyrannical visits and some of my father's insufferable relatives and the sympathy of neighbours and the constant, never-ending greeting of everyone who knew us: "Is Wull still idle?"

I know this for a fact because my father's family held a Burnside Buildings council one Saturday and made this proposition — they would pay his passage to New York so that he could join Allan, the youngest brother, and hopefully find work there if my mother would return to work in Glasgow *and* I would be dumped in a Home for Homeless Children. I learned years later that when she heard this proposal from my father, she got on a tramcar that night for Burnside Buildings and raised a Highland hell. She never went back to that house all her life.

Because my father was desperate, it was a touch-and-go proposition. I almost joined the élite of the homeless.

CHAPTER TWO

The Slump Years

To me the north side of this city of Glasgow was — and still is the last time I saw it — The End.

As a child it was a world of wild, cold blue skies reflected on the windows of grey tenements that stood in rows above the canal or off Maryhill Road in stark grimness. It was a world of the road-menders, tar-boilers and wee home dairies and the Co-op with sawdust on the floor and tramcars and drunken men on Saturdays and Mission Halls and old newspapers slapping around lamp-posts in the March winds. It was a cold world. I thought there could be nothing bleaker till I saw Springburn and Lambhill further to the north of the city.

Somehow the children in the nearby rougher streets around us shouted more, did more, were dirtier, happier and dangerous. We had no gang in Braeside Street. They did. The Kirkland Street midden-rakers terrorised everybody. We had no policeman at *our* corner. They did. They also had more drunks, shrieking women and broken windows. They got all the fun and all the punishment.

It couldn't have been the rents. (I think I remember my mother saying our room-and-kitchen was six shillings a week.) I think it was the people. We were quieter, more employed (except my father), cleaner and duller and slightly better dressed.

One of the most terrifying experiences I had was on Saturday morning fetching our groceries in a basket from the Co-op at Kelvinside Avenue. There was a lane that ran parallel to Maryhill Road which was a short cut home and this was the way I came. Then came the gang. There were about ten of them — mostly a family called Gallacher from the slum tenements on the main road — and they chased me right up that lane with the spoils of that morning's midden-raking: broken-off table legs, pieces of iron and blazing torches of bound-up canvas. There was a wooden barricade at the end of the lane over which I could comfortably climb into Stair Street and home. Not on this day. I nearly made it and just managed to save myself. Their lit torches got most of my mother's groceries. And that was the most serious thing to happen to us for months.

Frankly, I'm a bit tired listening to people who tell me that young hooligans are about the same as they always were, that the weapons have changed a little, that things haven't changed much among violent teenagers in a city like Glasgow. Those protagonists for "it's about the same as it always was" certainly don't have my memories of street life in Glasgow or they might agree with me that today's thuggery is infinitely worse and seems to be getting more savage every year.

The idea of any of the gangs around Maryhill Road when I was young carrying knives or hammers or chains was unthinkable. Violence — yes. Fights — of course.

But somehow these seemed to be more of the shouting and bashing variety than now. I had never even heard of the term "put the boot in" until after the war.

I am *not* saying the razor gangs didn't exist. Of course they did. With my own eyes I have seen a man being kicked half to death on a Partick pavement, a gang-fight with broken bottles and razors extending four tenement blocks in London Road, a bloody fight between four women in Springburn, and I remember even being threatened by a young man who opened his jacket to show me the rows of razors along his waistcoat pockets.

All I am saying is that the gangs of young teenagers then in Glasgow seemed to be content with firing middens, beating up other gangs and breaking windows. Old ladies were safe.

For the rest, life was fairly happy on the street. In a way, it was like a village settlement with Mrs McCleray's little all-things shop at the corner, the home-bakery on the other side of the hill and the well-tried and well-marked spots for games like Moshie and Release and Plunkers and Football with a tanner ba'.

"The Washie" was a domain in itself for the children in our street. Every back-court had a small, flat-roofed building consisting of a wash-house and a midden built side by side. And it was this flat — well, nearly flat — roof that lured the boys to crew the pirates' ship, defend the Foreign Legion fortress, man the stockade against Indians — or just to get up higher than anybody else.

You could do almost anything on a Washie except play on top of it when your mother was washing clothes inside it — not because it annoyed her but simply because the smoke belching out of the clay chimney-pot blackened your face and choked you. And the concrete roof got too hot for your feet. Washies in full power were formidable places.

"Rushing the Washie" was a great game. All it needed was four cowboys or knights or soldiers or sailors defending the roof with wooden swords or guns, and a few Indians, enemies, Germans or pirates scaling the sides — and that was another Ypres or Spanish Main or Bannockburn or Little Rock for an hour.

Much more hazardous was "Jumpin' the Washies" — and the best place for this was behind Oban Drive where the wash-houses were evenly spaced all along the back-courts. The spaces between the roofs were just short enough for a good leap and long enough to test the nerves of any boy. We only had one casualty when Andy Baillie misjudged his jump and landed in the dustbin below.

The worst thing I ever did on top of a wash-house was almost to asphyxiate Mrs Kelly, the big Irishwoman in Number 83. We knew she was in there all right. We had seen her carry her basket of clothes to be washed from the close-mouth across the back-court to the wash-house. And we knew she had lit the fire because the smoke was clouding out of the chimney right at my side.

I think it was Davie Archer who handed me the old newspaper he had got from the midden. "Here — pit that over it."

"Over what?" I said.

"The chimney. See whit happens."

I did. And it happened.

We saw the smoke belching out of the wash-house door, heard Mrs Kelly's Irish scream, saw her blackened face, and we got off that roof as fast as we could.

It was me she caught and my right ear was crimson from her slap for an hour afterwards.

I am no psychologist nor would I draw any conclusions from the phenomenon but there was considerably more clouting, slapping, hammering, thumping and pummelling of children when I was young. To be frank, I rarely had any of it. Two fights at school, half-a-dozen strappings by the teacher and three slaps which I remember from one of my harassed-to-death parents is about all the violence I remember — plus that deserved thump across the ear from Mrs Kelly.

However, matters of disagreement among and with children were often quickly and shockingly settled. Ginger Mac, the big Highland policeman who strolled up Braeside Street, would think nothing of slapping a boy's face if he was impudent. It was the "done thing". He also cut up rubber balls that came his way, purloined dangerous-looking toys like water-pistols and dragged many a malevolent boy by the ear to his mother's door. Nobody expected anything else.

Strapping at school was quite normal, quite expected by late-comers and "I-forgot-to-bring-it-sir" boys. Tears and jeers and red, swollen hands were absolutely usual.

What was the effect? Well, all I can remember was that most youngsters at school were always on time, sat up in classroom, kept quiet when the teacher was talking. Children on the street did not respect the policeman but they did fear him. And adults generally *were* respected.

It was a street that was never still because there were so many children. I think the reason for this was simply that couples all around the same age with babies settled there during and after the war so we were all growing up together. One of my happiest memories was wakening on the first Saturday of the school summer holidays and hearing already the yells and calls of other boys out on the street. This was the first day for shirts and white sandshoes — "sannies" — and the first of scores of running, shouting, exciting adventuresome days with bats and balls and marbles and comics and slings and broken-down prams made into go-carts. It was the start of new games and new explorations to the Botanic Gardens or jumping over the roofs of the wash-houses or discovering the labyrinth of cellars under the houses in Clouston Street.

I don't remember very much about the girls on our street — well, what boy *does* remember girls before he takes a real interest in them? All I can recollect of them in summertime were the prams, the dolls, the quieter "silly" games they seemed to play that had some connection with houses or hospitals or doctors or schools. Ugh!

What I *do* remember — and have never since forgotten — is that they were people never to be crossed, frustrated, argued with or teased beyond a certain point. Singly they were imponderable. *En masse* they were horrendous. Heaven help any boy in our street who got cornered by a crowd of girls if he broke up their game or upset a pram or kicked their peever.

15

Of course there *were* the odd Young Ladies — prim young things who *never* played peever, *never* bawled or screeched and never dressed up at Hallowe'en. I think I remember two of them — the Fulton sisters — and we were always a little in awe of them when they happened home and up their close from their fee-paid school in the West End.

It would be a very unfeeling person who would not be moved — even dreamy-eyed — about boyhood memories of wakening in the bedroom of a country cottage in summer, throwing open the window to the blue sky and listening to the glorious bird-songs.

I have boyhood memories of almost everything that was the reverse of that — yet fond ones that touch my heart.

No budding spring flowers or golden autumn leaves signified the seasons of the year in Maryhill. We had the city signs, the unmistakable, regular tokens that heralded the passing year.

March winds across the acid blue sky between the tenements showed us something of a springtime, certainly, but it was the starting up of street games like peever and moshie on the mottled wet-and-dry pavements that told us the dark days were over. Then the joyous toot-toot of the *Fairy Queen* told us the rest. This was a small pleasure-boat complete with awnings and flags and streamers that sailed all the way along the canal as far as Kilsyth then returned to Port Dundas in the city. It was a white, gay, chuggy-chug little boat that carried about fifty passengers, and when we saw its first appearance on the canal at the end of our street and heard its little tooting horn of triumph, we knew that spring *was* here. The passengers even threw pennies to the running boys on the canal bank to prove it.

Summertime was sanny-time, the season for wearing white sandshoes. It was also the time for making little balls from the soft tar on the hot, melting edge of the street. We had tarry knees and tarry hands and angry mothers (butter was the only thing that would remove it). It was summer, too, when we played and played and ran and ran with girds and hoops and home-made go-carts and balls and bicycles and barrows. The last tired child would be called in to bed from a first-floor window as the lilac of the evening sun was turning to night.

The autumn winds whistled through the back-courts and moaned through cold closes and up the stairs to the landings. Darkness came earlier; the children were fewer on the street; and something was missing now on the canal — the *Fairy Queen*'s cruises had ended for the year as the street-lamps were lit earlier and earlier.

Winters in Maryhill were wet and cold. Lonely chimneys squealed in the winds; even the tramcars on Maryhill Road moved tiredly and never rang their bells. Muffled-up children shuffled to the Dunard Street school round the corner and crowded into the sheds to escape the driving rains.

The first snow was a beautiful white carpet laid on every back-court, and we built snowmen and igloos and huge snowballs. On the street and on the main road it was a yellow slush that threw out sharply — like a Belgian winter-painting — the dark brown and black buildings and pavements and the starkness of the varnish works up on the canal.

But that first Saturday of the summer holidays from school seemed to me to be the first day of the world.

My mother called our back-court entertainers the Griddlers. I don't know where the name came from but I do know they were men — sometimes with a woman — who came round the back-courts of the tenements in summer and sang horribly in warbling, out-of-tune notes. The songs were things like "Marta — Rambling Rose of the Wildwood" and "Danny Boy" and "Mary o' Argyll". They were often down-at-heel men in frayed black coats and cloth bonnets and the women sometimes beside them poor-looking souls, bareheaded and sad-faced. It was usually when the woman started up her second-part harmony that you could hear a dog howling in the next building. The singing generally was excruciating.

Windows would open and some coppers wrapped in paper would be thrown over — more to get rid of the terrible singing than as a token of applause. I never heard anyone abusing them. Poverty was poverty.

By far the most interesting kind of back-street entertainer for me and my pals was the One Man Band. He was an event. It was usually the same man who came around our back-courts every spring and on each occasion he seemed to have added yet another instrument to his cacophony of foot-operated big drum, knee-bells, elbow-cymbals, tin-whistle, bones, kazoo and mouth-organ. He was a complete symphony of banging, blowing, jangling music and we stood gaping with amazement at his contortions in front of the midden. We followed him from close to close and back-court to back-court.

Sometimes we got a complete song-and-dance team in our street — four or five young men who played the dulcimer, the accordion and the saxophone while their pals gave us a step-dance. They wore navy-blue or plum-coloured cheap suits with narrow waists and padded shoulders, pointed shoes and natty little ties with dirty shirts.

As children we felt in awe of these fancy-stepping, confident-looking men who usually got showered with pennies from the windows of the tenements. They looked so self-assured, so competent. They were the "professionals".

Back in the 'twenties in Maryhill you had to be very discriminating with "hudgies". This was the sport of "hudging" a free ride on the back of lorries going up and down the main road.

In the first place you had to choose your spot for embarkation. If you waited on a suitable empty lorry at, say, Kirkland Street, there was a good chance of quick acceleration by the vehicle and you being thrown or dragged; that's how the road was at that spot. Kelvinside Avenue was different. The lorries always crawled there and you knew that once you had a grip of the end of the lorry you could get aboard.

Secondly, you had to choose your time of day.

I remember Andy Russell and me "hudging" a lift on a lorry going towards Milngavie at a quiet part of the day during school holidays. The road was quiet, too, and that driver belted along at a furious speed. When we passed the tram terminus we got alarmed and I banged on the driver's cab.

He stopped a mile beyond the city boundary, got out of his cab, and as we jumped off he yelled, "Ah hope ye enjoy the walk back!"

We didn't. It was three miles.

One of the strange things about being poor or underprivileged, I have found, is that you really don't know anything about it till somebody thirty years later tells you that you were poor and underprivileged. This makes me doubt the whole socio-economic value system today by which people are deemed to be "rich" or "poor". For my part, those days in Glasgow as the only son of an unemployed shipwright were happy. I enjoyed them. Of *course* we only remember the good things (what about that tuberculosis of the neck glands?); of *course* we don't remember ever being hungry (what caused that tuberculosis anyway?). And of *course* we don't remember ever being ill-clad. (Was it good fortune that gave me a mother who had been a tailor's seamstress and could convert an old coat into a pair of short trousers?)

You get used to anything. And sickness and even early death most working people accepted naturally in our street. Another thing everybody accepted quite readily was the conscientious but rather rough-and-ready medical care. If Mr McKay, the wee chemist in Maryhill Road, couldn't prescribe something to take away the pain, then a visit to the Panel Doctor was the next step.

Tuberculosis was a scourge in Glasgow. Whole

families were sometimes afflicted with it and it was quite usual to hear things like: "Ah hear he's married."

"Aye. Married that Campbell girl."

"She's a puir-looking soul last time I saw her."

"The whole family's peely-wally."

"Aye. Ye know what it is, of course. They're a' consumptive."

"It's in the family."

"Her brither died two years ago. An' the mither's been in decline for years."

"He's daft."

"The consumption" or "in decline" were the terms used for tuberculosis, and the pale, thin, pinched look of coughing young people was not unusual in any group in Glasgow. Highland people particularly suffered from this disease.

Even among my few relatives I can count three people who died of it before they were forty.

Children with "sore necks" were quite common. About the time I got my ration of poisoned neck-glands there were three other boys in the street also wearing bandages. They tell me that the main cause of *this* disease was untested milk.

The first operation I had for those wretched "swollen glands" was undertaken with chloroform on our kitchen table at home by Doctor Cameron, a small, dapper, kindly, efficient man. Another experience I remember was having my tonsils removed at West Graham Street clinic, wrapped in a blanket directly after the operation and carried by my mother on to a tramcar home, where, naturally, I was very sick. Rough and ready — but very practical.

I have formed the opinion that nearly all the changes we see around us — especially the unpleasant ones — are made by and for people over ten years of age. Under that age children don't want things changed from one generation to another — especially the sweets they eat.

Go into any confectioner's shop and take a look at what sweets are there for children. Mostly they are the same things you and I loved. Oh, they're dearer, yes — much dearer. Some of them are now packaged — yes; after all, who on earth would want to see the shopkeeper today make a cone-poke out of a piece of yesterday's newspaper? But the goodies are still there — liquorice balls, cinnamon balls, dolly mixtures, ju-jubes, sherbet "lunches", lollipops, sugar mice and treacle toffee.

One halfpennyworth was the ration in our street — and certainly not every day — and the Saturday penny was the Big Buy Day. I remember once buying a whole half-pound of broken biscuits from Dempster's the grocers with my Saturday penny and they lasted me all day.

Maybe you remember tiger nuts. You could buy a whole bag of them for a halfpenny. They were a rough-skinned little nut with no shell and they tasted sweet like coconut from their white insides.

The owners — usually motherly women — of "wee shops" made their own sweets. They made them in the back of the shop — toffee balls, ginger puff, coconut tablet — and it was quite usual to see a fresh metal tray of these goodies laid out on the counter, still warm from the making.

I was a very discriminating toffee-baller. I was daft about them and most Saturdays my penny went on a bag of them; some I kept over till a weekday, and a cheek bulging with a big, chewy gob of toffee was paradise for me around the age of seven.

There were as many vintages and types of toffee balls in as many wee shops around Maryhill as there were stars in the sky. Mrs Dobbie's in Dunard Street were the absolute best — the real large, handleable, non-stick, four-a-halfpenny gob-stopper. I experimented with others like Mrs Foster's in Northpark Street or Chambers's Wee Store in Napiershall Street, but these were usually too hard, non-melting, too small or too carelessly drawn for my liking.

Some wee shops got quite daring with their toffee balls by trying to introduce strips of coloured stuff through them or even coffee-coloured ginger strips round the edges but no toffee-ball maker could possibly camouflage a too-hard, too-brittle sweet with a mere striping of green or white peppermint flavour. A toffee ball was either a big chewy delight or it wasn't.

The Slump years, for all the poverty and privation, surely had many bright spots and advantages in a mining village because *everybody* there was unemployed. All were in the same boat and I knew that in many of the small, bleak little colliery communities outside Glasgow the pattern of plurality was the same. Everybody ran up debt with the local Co-op or the store; everybody helped everybody else; everybody knew everyone else's misfortune to the last penny. There was no stigma, no recrimination, no maudlin sympathy. It was a plural society in suffering.

Things were different for us in a place like Braeside Street because some people were working and others not. There were different scales of pay coming into different houses and we even had three boys and the Fulton sisters who went to a fee-paid private school over in the West End.

I need hardly say at which end of the social-economic scale we were positioned.

Good and bad, however, my life in that little side street off Maryhill Road was pleasant, noisy, competitive and it treated me kindly.

Heaven knows how it treated my mother. Highland pride, Scottish respectability and keeping up appearances in the face of hideous economic pressures would have driven a stable, educated woman insane. What it did to her who could barely understand the Co-operative Dividend Scheme must have been unthinkable.

CHAPTER
THREE

Moving Up, Moving Down

I must have been about six when we moved across the street to a bigger house. It had two rooms. It also had a lobby and a very clean lavatory on the half-landing of the stairway.

You really had to see a removal from a room-and-kitchen house in a Glasgow tenement to realise how few goods and chattels people owned. They usually filled a coal-cart with room to spare for the bird-cage and the two rolls of linoleum.

As far as I remember our wealth of furniture and fittings, carefully scraped and saved for over years, was a wardrobe, chest of drawers, two tables, four chairs, a medicine cabinet and a couple of dozen odds and ends like Dad's tool box, a shaving mirror, crockery, cutlery and ridiculous things like a goldfish bowl and Aunt Marian's soup tureen.

Everything had its place in our house. You would *never* find the hammer anywhere but in the kitchen dresser drawer, Uncle Roddy's wartime photograph but in the bottom drawer of the wardrobe, the washhouse key but on the nail behind the kitchen door or my schoolbag but hanging on the adjacent hook. Even in the busiest, most disordered house in the street there *were* limits to carelessness because there was simply no room for chaos.

There was the benefit of familiarity and speed about a wee place with few possessions.

No hunting in attics for sledges, cricket bats or old model railways was ever necessary because there was no attic and no old things. Spring cleaning was easy and simple. Books were got from the local library; toys were swopped with other children or destroyed at the end of the "season"; newspapers lit the morning fires or protected the freshly-washed kitchen floor; the few "survival" documents like birth certificates, insurance cards, the rent book and the co-operative dividend book were all safe in mother's large handbag in the wardrobe.

No wonder we never heard of a burglary of a tenement house. It wasn't worth it.

Number seventy-two was a nice stairway — no broken windows, no dirt, no bad smells — a respectable three-to-a-landing community of people ranging from the Hendersons next door, whose lanky daughter Joan was a nurse in the Western Infirmary, to wee Mr Robertson the painter in the single-end house in the close whose wife was a large, lumbering, careless, affectionate Highland woman who barely spoke English. She and my mother enjoyed each other's Gaelic lack of privilege among the respectable Lowlanders.

The rest of the people up that stairway — all twelve

families of them — we rarely saw. They were typical of the street — quiet, self-effacing and self-contained.

The boys I played with were the Hunters and the Mackies and the Baillies and the Russells. Many of the things we played with could nearly all be bought at Mrs McCleray's wee shop — peeries and marbles and chalk and tanner balls, and somehow somebody always had a few coppers to buy them.

When the Corporation of Glasgow Lighting Department did away with the gas-lit street lamps it is highly probable they removed one of the best playthings Glasgow boys ever had.

When I was very young I remember that they were so useful for everything in the world that was important to children. We climbed up them, did acrobatics on them, used them as goal-spaces in football, ran races around them — and sometimes accidentally broke the glass. Lamp posts in our street, it seemed, were put there specially for us and their purpose in illuminating the pavements with greeny glare at night seemed incidental.

No boy had "passed his colours" until — usually in front of an audience of lollipop-sucking girls — he had climbed the slippery cast-iron, ferruled pole, caught hold of the smooth cast-iron crosspiece, hung there for a few seconds' effect like a trapeze artist, then eased himself up till his chin touched the glass. There was usually a smell of gas.

The wee lamplighter always came round at dusk with his wee ladder and his wee pole. Somehow he was always a small man in a neat uniform and we used to watch him as he deftly used his pole with a gadget on the end to open the underside of the lamp which somehow switched on the gas and — plunk! — the lamp was lit in its green-white magic.

Yes, we broke the glass, too — never maliciously, never on purpose. It was always an accident — a too-high goal-kick by a badly-aiming boy or a misplaced catapult shot. The glass would crash, then tinkle and we would stand around in open-mouthed silence before we ran for the cover of the back-court.

They say that children are very cruel to each other. And the place where we see this most is in a school playground. The last time I watched children playing there did nothing to assure me that times have changed or that young human beings are any different from one generation to the next. Only the clothes, hairstyles and the things they talk about have altered.

When I was a boy at Dunard Street School I didn't want to fight, bully, or scream at anyone. I just wanted to be left alone. What I could not understand — and still cannot — is *why* boys must shove, elbow, strike, cuff and brawl their way to self-assurance. It's animal, I know, but it is not too much to expect that humans might have developed other traits in growing up.

One thing I *have* learned about aggression. It does not disappear or lessen with age. All that seems to happen is that men and women develop more cunning, learn to conceal their aggression drives under a façade of serenity and learn how to use their faces and voices to deceive others. Many of them — too many — are still, underneath, the same lashing, bashing, screaming youngsters I mixed with at Dunard Street school.

It is very likely that the teachers in the hideout of the staffroom had exactly the same drives under their barbed smiles and catty compliments about each other.

It is no surprise to me that television cartoons showing a gang of alley-cats and featuring one Top Cat who outsmarts everybody are so popular. I feel sure every city street has one in human form — the Big One, the Boy who Knows What's What.

Ours was a lad called Archie Hunter. He was tall, gangly, loud-voiced, brown-eyed and fearless. Everybody followed Archie. When the season of change from marbles to football happened, Archie was first. He was first with water-pistols, fireworks, cigarette cards and catapults. He was always last in being blamed for anything, buying anything and going errands for his mother. He was the Boyo.

Saturday morning games in the street never really got started till Archie appeared, running out of his close as if appearing on stage. He always began: "Ah'll tell ye whit we're goin' to do," and in three minutes we would be playing Moshie or Rounders or Rubbishy just as he said. He was the ideas boy — loud-voiced, undemocratic, charismatic and a winner at everything. If group behaviour has anything to do with future career development, I would not be surprised to know that the Boyo is now chairman of some huge enterprise.

You would think that most of the things children buy with their pocket-money are to be found in — well, *what* kind of shop? These days I've lost the place. Oh, yes — the ice-cream shop or the sweet-shop, certainly. But what about the other things — the gadgets and pocket toys and "crazes"? Or do they still have them?

When I was about eight Mrs McCleray's wee stationer's and "all-things" shop was all right for peevers and peeries, water-pistols and whistles, candle-lamps and chalk, dabbities, bangers, rubber balls, tin whistles and comics. But there was a whole galaxy of other things — some of them forbidden or at least frowned on — and these we got from Mr McKie's, the chemist.

Somehow the things you could buy in *his* shop were different — even the sweets. Of course there were the cough-drops and throat ju-jubes and sticks of liquorice and barley-sugar; these were ordinary enough even although you couldn't buy them elsewhere. But I remember best the "sinful" things like the brown sticks of cinnamon we smoked in the back-close, the halfpenny glass tubes that made the most devastating pea-shooters ever invented, the saltpetre and some other chemical we used as bangers for explosions outside the wash-houses and the rubber tubing that swelled up to a sausage-shaped, powerful water-cannon.

I always remember Archie for starting this "thermo-meter" craze. It had nothing to do with thermometers — that was just the name we gave to the twelve-inch length of flexible rubber tubing we bought for a halfpenny in McKie's the chemist's. We didn't know any other name to describe the two-feet-long sausage into which it grew when we filled it to bursting-point with water at the kitchen tap. Archie started this weaponry and within a few days nearly every boy in the street was squirting long jets of water at everyone else.

I only once saw Archie get what the Americans call his cum-uppance — via the "thermometer". He used to hide the water-stretched "sausage" under his jacket and hold the taut end of it in his fingers like a nozzle. One day in the school playground he was approached by wee Mr Simpson, the teacher, in full view of the rest of us.

"What've you got there, Archie?"

"Who? Me?"

"Yes — there. Under your jacket."

Archie tried to hide the end between his fingers and — just for a second — accidentally released it. A thin jet of water hit Wee Simpson on the face. We gasped in horror as the teacher calmly wiped his face with a large white handkerchief.

Archie stared — horrified. Mr Simpson came nearer to him, took a pin from the edge of his jacket lapel and opened Archie's jacket just sufficiently to let him touch the long, torpedo-shaped bag of water. There was a dull, sloshy bang as it burst and we thought Archie was going to cry as the water soaked all over his chest and waist, slowly seeping through jersey and trousers. Archie's "thermometers" were always bigger than anyone else's and they carried twice as much water.

Next week we were playing cricket.

Yet for all the wild running with bats and dribbling with small balls and making bogies in summer, it is the winter of the cold wet nights and the toys of those dark times that I remember best. When the wild November winds came to a Glasgow tenement street and the rain slashed across the little windows of brown houses, there was little a boy could do but watch it or ask if his mother would light the gas so that he could read his dog-eared comics or go down to the close-mouth and hope one of his chums would play marbles in the back-close.

The rain would be gushing down the gutters and roaring as if in an echo-chamber into the stanks at the corner . . . the pavements wet and shiny . . . Occasionally through the fluffing wind you could hear the sad, faint squealing of a chimney-top turning in the storm, and the pewter-grey slates of roofs glistened even to a dark purple colour.

All the time the wind would be moaning through the close and bringing with it the spray of the street's downpour.

My winter playground was the greeny gaslit stairway leading up to our landing. There a few of us could sit after our tea for an hour or so and play with cigarette cards or little lamps with coloured glass containing a smoky candle, or lead soldiers from which the paint had long worn away, or an old toy magic lantern that projected slides of Charlie Chaplin on to the whitewashed wall of the half-landing.

"You'll catch your death of cold!"

"Are ye no' cold sittin' on that stair?"

Some door would open or somebody's parent would pass with a remark like that — and the group would break up to go home when it got too cold.

One thing haunted my childhood in that street — telling anybody whether my father was in or out of work. I could never understand why people like Mrs Baillie were always asking me this, nor could I understand why my mother got angry if I said I had told her. It seemed to be a secret obsession in our house and I didn't know the secret. Nobody ever told me what I *had* to say.

Usually, however, there was no need to say anything. My father's unemployment advertised itself the day a ship was launched on the Clyde. I can remember some of my chums running up to me about six o'clock saying: "That's yer father comin' up the street wi' his boax."

I went down the street towards Maryhill Road to meet him — a short, burly, bent man in blue overalls, carrying on his shoulder a huge wooden box heavy with his shipwright's tools. He would say nothing as we walked up the stairs. He would be breathing heavily and gasping with the strain of the box and I wouldn't know till later that night that he was "off". Then the neighbours would start their questions again.

"Was that yer father I saw carryin' his box on Friday?"

"Is yer daddy idle again, son?"

"Yer father's no idle *again*, is he?"

Really, we were misplaced in Maryhill. By all the traditional selection of people for areas and houses and work, we *should* have lived in one of those bleak, tenement rows somewhere along the Clyde — Govan or Partick or Whiteinch or Linthouse. These were the Clyde houses, the natural, understood fitness-to-purpose houses for the thousands of angle-ironsmiths, welders, caulkers, hole-borers, riveters, shipwrights, platers and riggers who teemed on to tramcars in countless grey dawns to shuffle in great cloth-capped crowds into the shipyards that lined the river on either side.

The Clyde — particularly right after the Great War

— was the jugular vein for Glasgow. It seemed as if everybody one way or another depended on that rattling, hammering, banging riverside for his living. Sprawling out all along the side streets from the main yards were the smaller firms making everything from brass porthole covers to lifebelts. And sprawling out from *them* were the hundreds of little shops and pubs and working men's restaurants.

Maryhill was northwards a long way from this river artery, although with the wind in the right direction from the west and a lull in the tramcar noises you *could* hear the distant chattering roar of a thousand riveters drifting over.

I am almost sure my father was the only Clyde man in our street. Nobody else's father was a shipwright or rigger or plater or red-leader or angle-ironsmith in the shipyards. They were railwaymen or postmen or water inspectors or mostly house joiners or painters for the Corporation.

As I learned from my harassed mother, they had "cushy" jobs. "Never a day idle!" she would say bitterly as she banged the lid on the soup-pot. "Don't know they're born. Sly as cats, they are! Yu'd think some of them owned the street!"

Today, even my own family can't quite understand why I discuss *everything* with them. I answer every question on every subject — what I earn, what we spend, insurance, mortgages, debts, credits, the state of the household — everything. I suppose it's an instinctive reaction to those days of mystery of my own childhood in the Street.

CHAPTER
FOUR

"This is the boy, Miss Nobel"

I've noticed this about human beings — if they have no poor to patronise, they'll invent one. Of course we were an ideal target for some well-meaning people in our street.

"Hello, son — is yer faither idle or did he get a joab?"

"Yer faither still lookin' for work, son?"

"Tell yer faither there's something in the papers about a new ship they're startin' at Fairfield's."

"Wid ye like a piece, son?"

This last was the savage one — delivered innocently by a well-meaning mother of one or other of my pals, when she was making up a sandwich to throw over the window to us.

The worst and the best of these innocent humiliators was a big, brawny woman called Mrs Malcolm, who had a mild-eyed, subservient husband and two obedient boys. The older boy, Andy, was a chum of mine. Mrs Malcolm had a loud, shrill voice that came straight from the communal brashness of a Lanark country village and she *always* asked me the same question when I was in her surgically-clean, bleak house.

I usually replied, "I — don't know."

"Ye don't know if he's *workin'*?"

"No, I — don't think so."

"I see him comin' in and oot. He canna be workin'?"

"No — he's not."

She was banging plates triumphantly on the table. "Sit doon here wi' Andy an' jist hi yer dinner wi' us. It's tripe."

Of course my mother got to know and that was that. Mrs Malcolm's shrill interrogations came to a quick end. She or her tripe were no match for my mother's Highland pride.

I remember once picking up two little blue tickets out of the little china jar on the mantelpiece.

"Where did you get these?" My mother grabbed them from me. She was glaring.

"In the wee joog."

"Ye've no right in there."

"I was just looking for a pencil. What *are* they?"

"You mind yer own business!"

Of course I found out later. They were pawn tickets. I'll never know now what agonising decision had caused her (it *would* be my mother) to take some treasured thing to a place she had never seen in her life before — a pawnbroker's.

I knew *why* my mother went "back to service" when I was about six or seven. I don't know *how* it was arranged. Either the Old Lady wrote to us in our room-and-kitchen house in Maryhill — which was highly unlikely — or my mother called on her at her big apartment house in Lauderdale Gardens and asked to be taken back. And that was *very* likely.

However it happened, my mother worked from nine till four in that quiet, clock-ticking, highly-polished, soft-carpeted place in the quietest part of the west side of the city.

I had never seen a house like that one in Lauderdale Gardens. It was a first-floor apartment house which you entered after walking up twelve stone steps and through a brightly-brassed, heavy oak double-door.

The hall was like nothing I had entered before in my life because I had never seen a funeral parlour. It smelled of furniture polish and mothballs and the parquet flooring shone around two very expensive-looking, thick carpets.

There were five rooms in the flat plus a real, old-fashioned, scrupulously neat pantry. The "front" room was like a small museum with all sorts of carved, moulded, hammered, filigreed, beaten, bronzed and beaded objects from the East. There were miniature elephants, giant oyster-shells, tiny vases and enormous lamps hanging, sitting on or decorating the massive mantelpiece, piano and coffee tables.

The Old Lady was called Miss Nobel and for a long, long time she was just somebody my parents talked about. She was almost a myth. I walked all the way across the West End after school most evenings to meet my mother in the Lauderdale Gardens flat, tip-toed through the high hall and sat patiently in the pantry with a glass of milk in my hand until my mother had finished the sweeping or polishing or dusting or washing or burnishing the deadly-dark, sepulchral furniture and countless ornaments.

We certainly walked more then than I have seen people walk today. Now that I think of it, there was simply no way for me to get from Braeside Street on the north side of the city over to the West End where Miss Nobel lived except by walking. And *that* meant my mother walked too. Somehow we never thought twice about it. Five miles was nothing.

I remember my mother telling me that *her* father — the foreman boilermaker on the Clyde — walked every day to and from his work from their tenement house in Kelvin Hall Street to Babcock and Wilcox in Renfrew — and *that* was ten miles!

People walked everywhere and a job was a job.

Now that I think of it, even if my mother and I *had* tried to get public transport to Miss Nobel's place, it would have meant changing tramcars twice, cost a fortune and taken over an hour.

"Where is she?" I whispered one evening in the morning-room.

"Who?"

"The Old Lady."

My mother laughed. "She's away."

"Where?"

"Abroad."

"Where?"

"India or China or one of those places."

There was a photograph of her on top of the black

writing desk in the lounge. She was dressed just as I had seen Queen Victoria's pictures, and she had the same kind of drooping mouth and stern look about her eyes. I felt afraid of her.

The great day came when I met her. That evening at four o'clock when I rang the bell as usual and my mother opened the door, I knew something was different. She put a finger to her lips and drew me inside quickly. "Be very quiet," she whispered. "Miss Nobel's here."

"What'll I do?" I whispered, trying to tip-toe on the hall floor.

"Wait in the pantry. Don't touch anything. Just sit still."

I crept to the pantry and closed the door quietly behind me. I sat on the one chair in the little room and waited breathlessly.

Then I heard a door closing . . . some voices . . .

My mother, wide-eyed with excitement, opened the pantry door and said in hushed agitation, "Ye've to come in an' say howdyedo to Miss Nobel. How's your face? Is it clean? And your hair! Tch! Look at it! Now . . ." She led the way, flustering: "Jist for a minnit. Says she wants tae see you."

I followed my mother into the huge morning-room. Over at the window sat an old woman wearing a dark brown dress. She had greying hair and slightly bleary eyes, and was having tea from a silver tray on a table.

Miss Nobel lives in my mind yet, and if I were asked to describe her I would think of her as a vague, pale-faced, melancholy person who had a lot of money, a creaky, polished old house and who spoke so that only her friends, I expect, could understand her. She was tall, thin and grey.

My boots creaked on the floor as my mother gently pushed me towards the Old Lady. "This is the boy, Miss Nobel."

She looked at me, her hand holding the fine china cup. "Well, young man." There was the faint wintry smile of an aged spinster's attempt to be kind.

"Good evening, Miss Nobel," I said.

"Good evening to you." She reached down by her side. "I *have* something here for you, Roddy. Your mother tells me you read a lot. *Do* you read?"

"Yes, ma'am."

She held six copies of thin, blue-coloured magazines in her hand. "I want you to read these and you tell me what you think of them next time you're here. Mm?"

"Thank you, Miss Nobel."

I shook hands and tip-toed out in my squeaky boots clutching the slim magazines.

They were old copies of *Ashore and Afloat*, the monthly journals of the Mission to Seamen, containing mainly the list of donors and the annual balance sheet.

I felt much more comfortable reading the *Rover* at home.

The days of my father's unemployment were the days of him sitting at the window reading Dickens or Scott or Karl Marx, the days of strange, bitter silences in the house when my mother — as if by tight-lipped contradiction to idleness — worked harder and more noisily, scrubbed furiously at the front doorstep, swept the landing and stairway violently, banged doors and rasped: "Mind yer feet!" Angry, loveless days. The last and longest period of unemployment that saw me into my early teens was three-and-a-half years.

You hear a lot of talk today about this thing called "parental influence" and of how the lack of it at home is very harmful to the child. I wouldn't dispute this for a minute with the harassed policemen, the frustrated social workers and school teachers at the end of their tether trying to get parents to take an interest in their children. Indeed, you sometimes get the impression today that the child is competing so much for his parents' attention with television, bingo, clubs, mothers out working and the whole frenzy of a busy, pleasure-loving life that it is no wonder he turns to mischief to attract attention.

We had a very good cure for this sort of thing in the late 'twenties and it was built into the whole social and economic life of working-class people. It was called unemployment — and for all the horror this word conjures today in the minds of zealous politicians it had a lot of happy advantages for some children.

For a start, I saw my father and my mother every day and nearly all day. A father's influence? It almost smothered me just because he was there all the time — except for the few hours he was away looking for work. We did crosswords together, played draughts together, talked together. I never knew what a latch-key looked like, and if I had ever knocked on our door and there was nobody in the house I would have felt sure my parents had died. The house was a nest, a den, and it was always alive, populated by at least two out of the three of us all day, every day.

Washing day at our little house in Braeside Street was washing *night* simply because my mother couldn't be in two places at once and her days were spent "in service" looking after the Old Lady's place. So the weekly wash was done by her in the wash-house in the back-court some time after eight o'clock.

For her it must have been a cold, damp drudgery — carrying the basket up and down the stairs, lighting the fire in the brick-built stove on a dark winter night and scrubbing the clothes against a washing-board by the light of two candles. For me it was something different. I enjoyed washing night because it meant I could stay up a little longer, go down to see her and talk to her, come upstairs again and talk to my father.

I remember washing night, however, for another reason — I learned about Communism. I didn't particularly *like* listening to my father singing out of tune the "Red Flag" and the "Internationale" while my mother was downstairs but at least it got us together. It was on those nights he told me about strange things like "Workers of the World Unite. You've Nothing to Lose but your Chains," and what a grand martyr was John McLean and a thing called "The Dictatorship of the Proletariat" and "It's Comin' Yet for A'That," and the Tolpuddle Martyrs.

Looking back now I would say that my father's early attempts at teaching me political economy were based on a misty-eyed zeal for the thoughts of men called Lenin, Karl Marx, Rabbie Burns and That Traitor Ramsay McDonald. It was a very mixed-up, sing-songing session once a week. But I enjoyed them because I could go to bed later.

If a publisher in Glasgow in the early 'thirties had decided to print a daily newspaper which contained only the bad news, the man who would ideally have been its editor was my father. He had a genius for finding the gloom and doom in news.

I can remember him sitting by the fireside in our kitchen with the *Evening Times* open and searching through the pages for things like "I see they're shuttin' doon that furniture factory at Andersons. That'll be another thoosand men on the dole."

My mother would be ironing. "My, my! Again!"

Then there would be a pause while he did some more searching until he found another gem.

"Ah see the railwaymen are goin' tae let the miners doon again."

"Aye, they're a bunch, they are! Sly as cats."

"An' here's that case o' the faither in Govan that murdered his three weans."

"Tch! Tch!"

"Aye, aye — it's the times we're livin' in."

"It's a fact."

Sometimes, usually casually as if she did not expect any good news, my mother would ask, "Nae sign o' mair boats bein' built on the Clyde?"

"No. It'll be a long time afore *that* happens."

"Ah thought they were daein' somethin' with these government orders — warships or somethin'."

"Och, that was jist a sop." He would sigh. "A sop for the workers tae keep them quiet."

"But *wis* there warships?"

"Aye — one or two. But they went tae Merseyside. An' there was a submarine order for Newcastle."

"Nothin' for the Clyde."

"Naw — nothin'."

The tablecloth used for meals in our kitchen was usually a days-old copy of the pages of the *Evening Times*, and I have seen my father actually looking down the columns on the table while we were at tea to see if he could find some gloomy snippet he might have missed.

He usually found it.

In the early 'twenties it was the time of the crystal set — and not every family in our street had one of these — certainly not us. I remember the Russells had one — well, Mr Russell was knacky man, anyway, and he seemed to have everything new. After all, he was a joiner so it was no surprise to go into the Russell kitchen any evening and see the wonders of him footling around with a mysterious-looking little wooden cabinet and him wearing earphones listening to *radio*.

How the rest of us got our news was by the newspapers.

Catastrophes and crises came to us — usually late at night by the first distant sounds of a man calling something in Maryhill Road.

My mother would say, "Sh!", and as we poised in silence, straining our ears, we would hear again that mixed-up crying.

My father would open the window and we would hear the calling nearer. Then he would put on his jacket, go down to the corner and buy a copy of the late-special edition of the paper the man was selling.

I never remember him being disappointed. It usually *was* a catastrophe. There seemed to be no "trick" newspaper selling then. A late-special *was* late and it *was* special. The government had fallen or Drysdale's Chemical Works was on fire or the king had died.

One of the closest, happiest, noisiest families I have ever known belonged to wee Mr McKee and his wee wife. They had six children and he was a Clydeside red-leader who had been unemployed for six years. The children never had the slightest bother getting his or their mother's attention because paying attention to them *was* their whole job; they had no other employment.

Having an unemployed father had, as I say, many advantages. He was always there for talks by the kitchen window, to show my schoolwork or my drawings, to listen to little things I wrote. And I could listen to him telling stories or reading from a book. And he was always available for a walk, a "dauner doon the road".

It's a great pity he didn't fish or collect foreign stamps or have a bicycle; we could have expanded our whole father-and-son horizon on the dole. Poverty certainly bridged *our* generation gap.

I know he tried to get work. He and his pal Jimmy Kerr who stayed in the Arcade off Renfrew Street tried everything. Years later I learned about those wild and senseless explorations my Dad had with Jimmy — trying to sell bootlaces and knick-knacks round the doors in far-off districts of the city, following dray-carts filled with timber to see if they stopped where there might be a job for workers in wood, calling round the Clyde shipyards every other day where the green grass of industrial desolation was growing over the slipways and rabbits scampered around the rusting gear, tramping to one repair dockyard after another along the quays of a deserted, silent, cold river.

Then one day he stopped trying. That's the real terror of unemployment, so far as I can remember as an observer, not the lack of money (you get used to that), not the pawn-tickets, the meagre meals, the scrimping and scraping. The total destruction is the self-destruction — when a human being loses the will to work at all. And that, I am sure, is what happened to my father right up to the beginning of the war.

He was not even allowed to vegetate in peace by the window reading his books. Aunt Kate prevented that. By this time the black-eyed, shrill-voiced, almost witch-like spinster sister of my mother's was working as a nurses' help in a home for disabled children in Dunoon. She arrived at our room-and-kitchen house usually without warning to stay for any period from three hours to three days.

"Aye. Well. Ye're still here, I see."

"Hello, Kate." My mother would open the door to her nervously.

"Well, Will — any work yet?"

"Naw." My father would lay down his book.

"Well, d'ye know — I came up from the station in a tram and it was packed wi' men frae their work. Packed. Dungarees and toolbags." She would take off her coat and hat and sigh. "There's work for *some*, I can tell ye."

Of course I was too young to sense the acrimony, the criticism, the crude innuendoes that my Aunt Kate thrust into the air. All I did see were the trembling hands and the tears after she left.

CHAPTER
FIVE

The Forming of a Young Mind

While I would never suggest for a minute that the things a youngster reads around a certain age affect his or her outlook and thinking for the rest of life, there isn't much doubt, even among the experts, that it does something to the young mind. And I don't mean the classics or the poetry or the essays to which they are exposed in school. What I mean rather is the material most parents and teachers either ignore or frown upon — usually comic papers and the like.

Of course I read the comics either when my mother could afford to buy me one now and then, or if I could borrow some from my pals. At various stages I enjoyed *Tiger Tim* and the *Wizard* and the *Rover* and *Funny Wonder*. Only a few months ago I sent away an order for half a dozen of these comics to a firm in Manchester which specialises in out-of-date copies, and just for the fun of it, I bought those of the late 'twenties and early 'thirties. I was amazed at many things. In the first place, they seemed so crude; the drawings were dreadful, the captions idiotic and explanatory text matter at the foot of each picture so tiny I could barely read it.

Other things, too, surprised me. Generally the paper was rough and ill-cut. And some of the comics — like *Comic Cuts*, were printed on tinted paper, pink or green or blue which made the reading even more difficult. Yet I can never remember having the slightest difficulty with these problems when I was seven or eight. As I got a bit older, the ones which attracted me more were the "schoolboy" type like the *Magnet*. I used to get these handed down to me from other boys, and I loved the Harry Wharton stories with Billy Bunter and the rest. Great stuff.

Where I seemed to "come of age" with my reading, however, was in the pages of a weekly newspaper of my father's called *Forward*. This was a left-wing organ with a wide circulation among working people in the West of Scotland. One of the most popular features occupied a page and it was called "The Judge". It showed a drawing of a bewigged judge seated on a bench with his clasped hands in front of him as he glared accusingly at some poor wretch in the dock opposite. There was a different "accused" every week — usually right-wing politicians or leading business figures — and the text occupying a full page consisted of an interrogation by the Judge, like this:

THE JUDGE: You will not deny, Mr Snodgrass, will you, that over the past three years you have been behind most of the rent increases in the poorer districts of Scotland?

SNODGRASS: Well, I wouldn't put it quite like that —

THE JUDGE: Allow me to present the evidence . . . And so on.

My father loved this sort of thing. In a way it was a little like Madame Defarge who kept knitting as the tumbrils brought one aristocrat after another to the guillotine. My father read with relish how one or other so-called tyrant or despot or crooked politician was dragged in front of the Judge in print every week and accused of his crimes in front of the whole world — or, at least, that part of the world in the West of Scotland which read the thing.

I forget what age I was when I first stumbled my way through the printed words on that page of *Forward* — possibly five or six — and when my father heard me mouthing the denouncing phrases he beamed in admiration. "Listen to that," he would say, "He can read."

"Aye — reading rubbish," my mother would say.

"You carry on, son."

Then I learned to intone the words and phrases like a street orator, and this amused my father even more. Later I learned to earn more approval by standing at the kitchen table and putting my hand on my chest and reading the Judge as if giving a speech. The most my mother would give by way of approval was "Ye'll wag yer heid in the pulpit yet, son".

Years later I actually saw the publisher and editor of *Forward*. His name was Guy Aldred and he had a little shop and printing press in George Street. That is where I saw him as he entered the place. He was a sallow-faced man with long hair and he wore breeks and long woollen stockings as if he had just returned from a hunting expedition. (Perhaps he had and his "bag" may well have been another dozen or so adherents to his cause.)

The kitchen table was a whole world in itself of printed pages. Our tablecloth, in any case, was always a copy of the Glasgow *Evening Times* except when we had a visitor whose presence was graced by a tablecloth. I remember the cartoon "Miffy" in the *Times* and "Jiggs" in the *Daily Record*. I never rested content until I could read all the captions, and I enjoyed repeating them to my parents. Sometimes I even read the main news events without understanding anything about what was going on in Britain.

The things we got to read at Dunard Street school were a bore. The standard Palmerston Readers were produced every morning and one boy or girl after another was instructed to read pages from it. None of it ever made any sense to me. There were no stories — certainly none that I could remember. Just words and stumbling recitations and a harassed teacher urging each pupil to "Well, get on with it".

That was the mind-boggling, yawning situation with school reading material at my school until Mr Simpson. He was our general teacher at that school and I formed the opinion one sunny afternoon, a week before the school closed for the summer holidays, that he was a genius. It was the custom then — probably still is — for things to slacken off around this time; lessons were relaxed and the teacher's main job, I expect, was to keep us amused or interested in something.

Mr Simpson decided to tell us a serial story. He had

a book open in front of him and he said he would read a part every day until the final day when the school closed. Then he started to read. I could hardly believe what I was hearing. It was a tremendous story — about a wee boy who lived with his mother in a tavern by the seaside called "The Admiral Benbow" Inn. What we were hearing was the story of *Treasure Island*. Most of us were open-mouthed and goggle-eyed — I certainly was — listening to Mr Simpson telling us all about Long John Silver and Black Spot and the voyage of that wonderful ship, the *Hispaniola*, as it sailed to this island of boyish dreams and adventure.

I could hardly wait to ask my father to get me a library ticket and I got the book out. From then on I devoured a mixter-maxter of literary meals almost every day of *Comic Cuts*, *The Swiss Family Robinson*, *Tiger Tim*, *Treasure Island*, the *Rover* and *Forward* plus items I could read in the newspapers. Far from getting mental indigestion, I loved them and saw nothing the least bit odd in mixing Chester Conklin and "His Adventures" in the *Funny Wonder* with Hans Andersen's *Fairy Tales*.

Books like *Treasure Island* seemed to fire me off like a cannon ball. My fuse lit again one day when my mother took me on my birthday to a matinée performance of the pantomime Aladdin at the Theatre Royal in Hope Street. I had never seen any play or people on a stage before. And this experience nearly knocked me out. I remember that the comedienne was Nelly Wallace. The costumes and the scenery and the music took me into a paradise that afternoon, and after we got home I drew pictures and even dressed up and gave little performances myself in our kitchen. Later I gave the same performance to a larger audience of Andy Russell and Jimmy Mackie and their sisters on the stairhead.

When I see on television today resurrected films from the 'twenties and 'thirties I wonder how on earth those of us who watched them in those days gathered any impression at all. The reproduction of these "rainy" scenes was — and still is — terrible. The actions now seem so jerky and lacking in any credibility. And the story-lines — well, I wonder if there was any story at all.

Yet those ridiculous cowboys in their big hats, and those restaurant waiters with their big moustaches and those fluttery-eyed girls lying on railway tracks must have made a big impression on us youngsters at the Saturday matinées. I know this because I joined in with the others in cheering and booing and yelling and whistling in the twopenny wooden seats in the Star cinema on Maryhill Road.

Of course there was Tom Mix and Buck Jones and Charlie Chaplin and Buster Keaton. In Glasgow the usual price at a Saturday matinée to see those wonderful people was either a penny or twopence, depending on the class of cinema. I went with my pals variously on a Saturday morning to the Seamore or the Blythswood or the Star. Very occasionally my father and mother took me to the little Gem cinema at St George's Cross where all the pictures somehow seemed to feature Clive Brooks. They were always very genteel films at the Gem. Also the seats were upholstered.

Now and then a film would come along which set

us going for weeks on the street dressing up like the leading characters in makeshift Foreign Legion garb or like Roman charioteers or British army soldiers in the trenches (old uniforms and haversacks and belts were never difficult to unearth in the early 'twenties so soon after the end of the war). The "cowboys and Indians" scene, of course, was endemic. Almost every back-court had its battles and stockades and ambushes. One of the most magnificent birthday gifts I ever received was a cowboy suit made for me by my mother from canvas sacking obtained from the Co-op grocery store.

One of the epic films that fired my imagination for months was a wartime naval thing called "The Battle of the Colonel and Falkland Islands". The sinking of one of the British battleships to the piano accompaniment of "Land of Hope and Glory" brought tears to my eyes.

Among the cartoons were Felix the Cat, Betty Boop and Mickey Mouse — silent, of course, but hurried along by the pianist. Sometimes we could even *see* this pianist dimly lit by her music light in the "pit". It was usually a middle-aged lady wearing spectacles.

CHAPTER
SIX

The Hielanders

They were an odd lot, these people on my mother's Highland side of the family. Maybe we didn't deserve generosity or understanding because we certainly didn't get it. I remember my father telling me how he and Jimmy Kerr heard that there was a slight chance of work for carpenters at the building of the new Electricity Board building in Waterloo Street. So they went down to the city and talked to the foreman, who said:

"Are ye construction carpenters?"

"Well — no."

"You're from the shipyards?"

"Yes. But we're desperate for a job."

The foreman thought about it. Then he said: "All right — start on Monday. But if ye're caught with shipwrights' cards I'll have to sack ye."

"We'll risk it."

So they started work. It was my father's first job in months.

My father didn't know that my mother's old Uncle Angus was on the same site working as a joiner, a construction joiner, a round peg in a round hole. Nor did he know that Angy was the union steward.

They met on a gangplank two storeys up the skeleton building and Angus, always smiling with his blue, twinkling, cunning Hebridean eyes, said:

"Well now — it's yourself, Wull!"

"Hello, Angus."

"My, my! Isn't this the limit, eh? Here's you an' me on the same building."

"Aye. I've been here three days. Got started on Monday."

"Man, man — you don't tell me! An' you a shipwright, eh? How did you get started, Wull?"

"I think the foreman was sorry for us. He said he'd give us a chance — me and my pal Jimmy Kerr."

"Did he, now? Well, well!"

They were fired that afternoon.

I was a child long enough ago in Glasgow to remember the Highland immigrants to the city and for better or worse was a grandson of two of these Gaels. Neither my grandfather nor my grandmother could speak a word of English when they came to Glasgow, and as my mother and her two sisters were from Stornoway, half my childhood was tinged with the Highlanders.

They were an odd lot — peasant-sly, tolerant of everything, the men either drunken or piously teetotal, the women servile, clannish, strangely kind in a spontaneous way, fearful of authority, greedy and often dirty; Glasgow was full of them. They were policemen, servant-girls, shipyard boilermakers, nurses in the city hospitals, labourers, tramcar drivers, church ministers and calf-eyed housewives. I never met any Gaelic shopkeepers, postmen, school-teachers, tramcar *conductors*, insurance men or rent collectors, although I did meet two who became world-famous in medicine.

My grandfather was the tallest, broadest and most formidable of all of them. For years he had been foreman boilermaker in a Clyde shipyard and he made big money and drank a lot. I remember my mother telling me that he employed a clerk to tally up the men's wages in McColl's Pub on Dumbarton Road across from the yard every Friday. Then my grandfather would dole it out to his gang. I doubt if he could read or write.

There's a white sheep in every family and on my mother's side that was Uncle Murdoch. Actually he was my mother's uncle but we all called him Uncle Maudo. I remember more of him on his knees praying than standing up, and when we visited him and his divorced daughter Bella and her son Robert in their wee house in Scotstoun we started praying — him on his knees — before they even put the kettle on for a cup of tea.

I don't remember ever meeting a more melancholy man. He seemed to be laden with doom and och-ochs and head-shaking and a long face.

Uncle Maudo was a tramcar driver, deeply grateful to have this dignified job and wearing his green uniform with grim pride. My mother told me that during the General Strike crowds of strikers tried to get him off his driver's platform but they failed. Uncle Maudo got his tramcar through to Shettleston.

He was a member of a small, Highland religious sect that met in the Bethel Hall round from Earlbank Avenue, and once he took me there. I remember sitting beside him and singing and praying and saying "Hallelujah" when he did. Everybody was miserable and they seemed to enjoy it.

The main characteristic I remember about my grandfather, my uncle Angus, my uncle Murdoch and all those Gaels in and out of our family was what my father called "playin' away at the thinkin'". Of course they were afraid — of each other, of being thrown out of work, of people with learning, of authority.

Even the sex of their pronouns got mixed up. "Is she in?" said a Highland policeman to a neighbour of ours enquiring about her son who had broken a window. Their conversation in our house was a good two hours of pipe-puffing, shifty-eyed, grinning nothingness.

"Och-och. That's the way of eet, then."

"Mm-mm. Chist so."

"Chist so."

"And you'll not be coming back there, then?"

"Och-no."

"Chist so."

"Mm-mm."

As children among ourselves we heard the Glasgow people call them "teuchters" and "Hielan' Stoats", mainly those who were jealous of their tenacity at keeping in constant, steady employment. Wages were low and the poorly-schooled Highlander knew his place and his worth.

The long overhead railway bridge over Argyle Street at Central Station was called "The Hielanman's Umbrella" because that is where they used to congregate on a Saturday night. The pubs were nearby; the whisky was a great depressant of fears and suspicions and you could hardly walk along the pavement among the crowds of Gaelic-speaking men — and a few women.

I believe every city in the world has a period when ignorant, wide-eyed people from a simpler life elsewhere swarm into it, populate its poorest quarters, take the menial jobs and congregate on Saturday nights somewhere where they can meet, drink and feel part of the human race again. It is the Germans in this decade who have tried to dignify such invasions with the term "guest worker".

When I was a boy I grew up at the tail-end of this invasion of the city of Glasgow, was part of it by birth and have lived long enough to see it mutate to something far less attractive.

Following the dray-carts — those long, low, horse-drawn vehicles that rumbled through Glasgow streets — *did* pay off, a few weeks after that. My father and Jimmy followed one to where it stopped at Firhill Football Ground. They talked to the foreman, who started them to work on the construction of the new grandstand. That job lasted ten months.

The first pay-day after my father started work was always happy. My mother was always waiting for him with her coat on so that she could go out and buy all kinds of the good things we hadn't seen in ages. I remember there was usually a melon or a coconut and some sweets for me. And I knew I wouldn't be seeing potatoes and salt herring again for a long time.

There's one comfortable thing about a good-going

slump. Everybody's in the same boat — maybe not all with *you* down below among the boilers, perhaps not in the third-class cabin accommodation, maybe not even sharing your cabin at all. But you're all on the same ship. And everybody's down two or three decks from where they were.

At least that's how I remember the slump in the late 'twenties. Anybody who was unemployed had plenty of company.

I can remember well in Glasgow the crowds of cloth-capped men standing, maybe a hundred at a time, at Anderston Cross or St George's Cross and certainly at Bridgeton Cross around the old bandstand. You could see them nearly any weekday from a tramcar. Just standing. Talking. Pontificating. Reading newspapers. Few laughed.

My father never stood around with crowds like this but he *was* one of them. It struck me years later that the men you heard about who *were* employed had kind of *specialised* jobs — sanitary inspectors or door-to-door insurance men or school janitors or dental mechanics — people like that. The unemployed were largely people like my father, who was a shipwright. They were usually hired *en masse* at yard gates — riveters and welders and riggers and red-lead painters — and they were the first and the longest to suffer during a slump. Hired as a mass — fired as a mass. Oh, yes, we did hear about Mr McManus the glass-blower or young Mr Neilson the pattern-maker being out of work, but it was usually only for a few months at the most.

It is hardly likely that a boy of ten would know

much about the bitterness and hatred of "the system" by the unemployed. But — and I must say this — the general memory I have of those I met with my father was that they were cheerful. Apathetic, some of them. But I cannot remember the hostile, angry scowls, the deep-seated bitter acrimony of disillusioned men that many speakers and writers of the 'twenties assure us was there in Glasgow.

Of course the hunger-marchers did not spring from a happy band of patriotic optimists — I know *that*. The occasional ugly scenes of troops and tanks in George Square we read about were not enacted by cheerful men who suddenly "got up to some mischief".

All I am saying is that the unemployed I occasionally met and watched and heard in my father's company were resigned to their lot and smiled as much as anybody else.

I often wonder how the politicians and labour leaders saw us in the early 'thirties — those of us in the working-class back streets. Yes, it was *us* they were talking about. I can tell that by going through old newspapers of those years. From what I read those grim-faced, frock-coated, concerned statesmen of conservative conscience and, on the other side, those blazing-eyed, stalwart champions of the poor and unemployed must *surely* have looked over their shoulders now and then to see the people whose miserable lot they swore to improve. Did they? I doubt it.

The truth of the matter is that, with a few exceptions like my Uncle Jock who was always spouting politics, none of us seemed to care. And I mean the adults.

Politicians were much the same as they are now, people in London who talk.

In the late 'twenties the world of politics to me was dictated by my father. There were Baddies and Goodies. To an unemployed shipwright, how on earth could people like Asquith and Baldwin and Churchill be good, honest, upright statesmen? It was unthinkable. They belonged to Group Number One — and they were all bad, all representing the Boss Class, therefore they would be all bad to me. They *must* be — my father said so.

Group Number Two, in his estimation, were the fence-sitters, the let-you-downers, the seller-outers, the pretenders to the faith of the working man, and I remember the names of Jimmy Thomas, Ramsay MacDonald, Philip Snowden and somebody called Ben Tillet ("Ben To Let" as my father said).

Then with bated breath and with hallowed expression came the names in Group Number Three — John Maclean, Jimmy Gallacher, Jimmy Maxton and Guy Aldred. This group were spoken of in the same tone as Lenin, Karl Marx, Rosa Luxembourg and Karl Liebrik.

I suppose if I took the trouble to go through files of the Glasgow newspapers from 1922 to 1932 I would probably see what really happened in our times then as they affected people like us in a remote district on the north side of Glasgow. Certainly I would be bound to read about the agonising problems of the unemployed, the economy and the rising tide of leftism that threatened to engulf all of us.

Seen through my father's eyes it was all just a matter

of time before those castigated and applauded political names were replaced by other names; then, he said, we would have something called the Dictatorship of the Proletariat.

CHAPTER
SEVEN

Doing the Rounds in Religion

Braeside Street had one great advantage for couples with young families — the school was just round the corner. It was called Dunard Street Elementary and that's where I went.

It was a plain school — simple and solid and no-nonsense. As it backed on to the rear of Braeside Street, my mother could pass me my "play-piece" of bread and jam at eleven o'clock through the railings.

I can never remember doing anything very well at school. I was a sort of nondescript boy whom nobody noticed, gave no trouble and never achieved much. In fact I had a look, the other day, at the one and only school photograph I ever had taken at that school and I had a task finding myself. It must have been a greater task for others.

Somehow we don't remember the nice teachers. The ones we remember — even brag about — are the tyrants, the beetle-browed, tight-lipped strapwallopers who put us to work and kept our noses down.

The ones I remember best were a mixture of

personalities but *none* of them were nice or naïve or nervous. And I remember them — as I expect you do *your* star teachers — for one particular incident in a young life.

The heftiest and sorest strapping I ever got was from Mrs McDonald, a tight-lipped, rimless-spectacled lady with her hair caught in a bun. And I got it because of half a pound of barley. Well, you remember what we used barley for, don't you? Didn't you spit it through a peashooter? Somehow I had a whole half-pound bag of it one afternoon and naturally when she went out of the classroom we delved into my barley and were spitting it through glass tubular peashooters (a halfpenny in McKie's the chemists). So far so good.

Then I took the bag of barley out to the front of the class — I can't remember why — and it burst. The grains scattered in thousands over the floor and it was so slippery you couldn't stand on your feet.

Neither could Miss McDonald when she came back. She went straight back with her legs in the air.

It was *my* bag of barley. And it was me to be punished. By the end of that strapping I am sure her right bicep was stiff. I know my right hand was like red pulp at the end of the revenge session.

As for my parents, they never asked me much about school, never urged me to any homework (I don't believe I had any), and took very little interest in why I was at school at all.

I looked forward to the day when I would qualify for the Big School. That was North Kelvinside Secondary up in Oban Drive where the Clever Ones were, where they taught the Big subjects like mathematics and French and algebra and art.

There was once a fight in the open ground just down from our school between a big, muscular chap from Firhill and a wee skinny boy called Lumpy.

The boy who was with me among the crowd watching this massacre was Jackie Monahan whose family had just returned to our district from New York because the father had been killed working on a skyscraper construction site. They had been in America only a year but this was enough to give Jackie all the pose and accent of a cowboy. After watching Lumpy being knocked down for the third time, Jackie pushed his way through the crowd of shouting boys and put his hands out, separating the fighters. There was a hush as he drawled just like Tom Mix or John Wayne, "Now wairra minute, stranger." He looked at the big lad from Firhill. "This li'l feller ain't no match for you." He raised his finger against the big lad's face. "Before you hit him again — jest hit me *once*. Jest once."

The big fellow hit him. We heard the "clunk" of his fist on Jackie's jaw and saw him fall down — right down, full length.

It took us all of five minutes to get Jackie back to consciousness at the school well with lashings of cold water and face-slapping.

He never spoke about the fight — ever.

There's a lot of nonsense talked about children going on holidays. Somehow it *must* be the seaside, there *must* be sunshine and there *should* be donkey-rides and ice cream and bathing and games on the beach.

This is no recent thing. Long before the Majorcas and

Costa del Sols and Jerseys when I was a boy there were still the same kinds of holiday posters showing children building sandcastles, and stories in the magazines of Eric and Elsie exploring the caves at the cove. In fact collections were taken around the schools for the Poor Children's Holiday Fund and the Fresh Air Fortnight for Orphans. Every child — even in the poor late 'twenties — *had* to have a week or a fortnight by the sea. You would have thought that any child who didn't have a few days by the bracing sea would die pale and panting in the foetid city before winter.

I had my annual holidays in Coatbridge. And it did me the world of good.

Coatbridge was a small mining and steelworks town twenty miles from Glasgow and in places it looked just like Glasgow except it had more smells, more smoke, was noisier and the canal ran through the middle of it. The place where I stayed was my aunt's house in a little, dull, respectable side-street with grey terraced houses and a common backyard that served most of them round a square. At the back the houses looked like colliers' rows; from the front they looked coy and genteel.

The first time my mother took me through to Aunt Marian and Uncle Jim and Cousin Kirsty in Coatbridge we got the tramcar as far as Baillieston, then were taken by an open-top motor-car from there to Coatbridge. I believe the fare on the motor-car was threepence each.

I remember seeing the Coatbridge Canal and the silhouette of the blast furnaces and the pit and the hanging pall of yellowish mist, and smelling the sulphury tang from the steelworks. And for years afterwards I thought that all holiday resorts had these features.

I really enjoyed those two weeks at Coatbridge. My uncle was a baker and Kirsty and I used to run round to the main road before breakfast to meet him — white as a snowman — and each take his hand and smell the aroma of the bread and rolls and scones and cakes he had just baked. We were very happy. I met new friends and played new games. It gave me great pride to teach the other children some of the Glasgow street games they never knew. I also had some quite new experiences like going to church and filling my uncle's pipe and shaking hands with visitors and playing snakes and ladders.

Somehow the children in that street seemed so ruddy and healthy. They were robust and loud, with bright eyes and apple-cheeks. I remember my uncle saying it was the fumes from the steelworks that kept everybody healthy — and I still believe he might have been right. I saw no bandaged necks or rickety legs or consumptive faces in that canal-reeking, sulphur-smelling little Lanarkshire town any time during my holiday. And I know I returned home every summer very healthy and braced up.

Nearer the beginning of this century Yorkhill Sick Children's Hospital in Glasgow had an arrangement with a convalescent home at Ravenscraig near Inverkip on the high hills beyond Greenock whereby poor children could be sent there after an operation to "brace them up." I caught up with this arrangement in 1925, when I was eight, after an operation to the glands of my neck, and my parents agreed to have me sent to the home.

It was a big, old-fashioned, grey country house set in

the middle of a meadow with a driveway going up to it. There were about twenty boys and girls in the place all dressed more or less uniformly in little grey trousers or skirt and red-and-white striped blouses. Those children who were suspected of having lice had their heads shaved. The others — I was one of them — simply had their heads cropped, leaving a little "brush" above the forehead. The "brush" children therefore constituted at once another "class".

The home was run by two middle-aged women — a Matron with a hooked nose and a fat Sister with a scowl and thick glasses. They were assisted by a young Greenock girl who was the only kind person in the place.

This maid — her name was Vera — amused us down at the little shed by the playfield by singing popular songs. The way she sang, "Marta — Rambling Rose of the Wildwood" had all the nasal, glottal-stop twang of a Glasgow street singer but she *did* sing in tune and every other line ended with a heartbreaking sob. "All My Souvenirs" was sung with her mouth slightly askew for effect. "You're the Cream in my Coffee" was shoulder-shuffled. "Ramona" had her eyes closed as if she couldn't bear to hear the sad tale. And "All Alone by the Telephone" was the most pathetic thing I had ever heard in my young life.

Of course, although Vera's songs were always in tune, musically they were completely out of tune with the age-group of those gawking, thumb-sucking, wide-eyed seven-year-olds. The boys wanted "Tipperary" and the girls "I'm Forever Blowing Bubbles". Instead, all of us got "Ma, He's Makin' Eyes at Me" and "The Rose of Tralee" whether we liked it or not.

I remember waiting and waiting for days for my mother and father to visit me. And I remember trying not to cry.

One day — it must have been visiting day — they actually arrived. It was wet, and with the other parents and children we met in the wooden-floored day-room for a precious hour.

After everyone had gone the Matron sent for me and in her office she towered over me bustily.

"Wilkinson, were your parents here today?"

"Yes, ma'am."

"Did you see the footmarks they left on the day-room floor?"

"No, ma'am."

"You *didn't*? Come with me, boy."

I followed her into the large, floor-polished room and saw the hundreds of drying footmarks of dozens of sodden feet.

"There," she said, pointing.

"My parents?"

"Yours — and the rest. Get a bucket of water and soap and a cloth and I want to see that floor thoroughly cleaned before supper." She clapped her fat hands. "If it is *not* done — you get a beating."

I washed it all — every strip of that oak floor, every corner, every cranny — and went in to supper to hear the jeers and yells of the striped-bloused children.

* * *

I "did the rounds" with religion. My mother got the notion that because she had had me christened at the age of two months in Queen's Cross Church, that service would somehow serve my spiritual needs for the rest of my life. And I suppose it might have done so if I hadn't palled up with Andy Russell next door. His family were an odd lot with their worship and somehow I found myself in the Evangelical Hall at St George's Cross with them. I was about seven at the time and all I can remember was loud singing and Hallelujahs and some girls with tambourines and men in blue serge suits and creaky boots.

The next place of worship — for two Sundays only — was with my mother and a Highland cousin of hers at the Gaelic Church near Kelvinbridge. I doubt if I could have understood it even if the service *had* been in English.

Joining the Boys' Brigade and the Sunday School at the little church down the hill at Yarrow Gardens was about the nearest I ever came to what might have been a fairly usual, ordinary religious service. I know I enjoyed the Church Parades and the Sunday School annual trip but I don't remember anything about the church.

What I do remember sharply was later rejoining the Russell family in their evangelical adventures — this time to the Church of the Jehovah's Witnesses in St Andrew's Hall in the city. That *was* a masterpiece of boredom. Andy and I used to sit at the back of the hall and with others in the congregation listen to the dullest, droniest voice I had ever heard of a man called Judge Rutherford, played on gramophone records.

It was about this time my father suggested that maybe my Sundays might be better spent at the Socialist Sunday School but one howl of protest from my mother silenced him for ever on *that* subject. In any case by this time I had joined Grove Street Institute with Alex Redpath and Johnny Ryan.

Grove Street was a long, wide, desolate street of grey tenements that stretched from St George's Road through to Garscube Road. Halfway along it was the Institute, a huge Greek-style building with steps and pillars and nooks and crannies carved from stone, all of which provided a soot-grey background to an enormous white linen banner that carried a religious message.

It was Alex Redpath, a boy in my class at school, who invited me to attend the Institute on Saturday nights. The value for money was fantastic. For one penny you got a cup of tea, two Paris buns, a lantern-lecture with coloured slides, the Silver Band, six hymns and a bang-up show from the stage on the evils of drink or a drama about betting on horses.

I would never go so far as to say that our Saturday nights at Grove Street Institute improved our spiritual awareness one whit. That would be an exaggeration.

What *was* true was that Alex Redpath, Johnny Ryan, his sister Jenny and I enjoyed ourselves thoroughly. There was so much going on — a silver band, a lantern-lecture, a fire-and-thunder sermon from a man in a blue serge suit, a cup of tea and two buns, and at least five rip-roaring hymns. All for twopence.

Of *course* Johnny Ryan made a waggling rabbit shape with his hands in front of the slide projector.

Of *course* Jenny dropped her bag with one half-eaten bun in its bag over the balcony. Naturally. And Alex Redpath would have considered the evening a failure if he hadn't hummed "Shall We Gather at the River?" through a paper and comb while the band played.

But, all in all, it was pretty harmless fun and — looking back now — did little to divert the attention of the two or three hundred people from their devotions.

It was no accident that Grove Street Institute was situated right in the middle of the greatest congregation of pubs and fish-and-chip shops and screaming, squalid tenements imaginable. Saturday night when the Institute emptied was for me a hullabaloo of the silver band playing and drunken men on the pavements and packed streets and shouting, fighting people and barrow-men selling roasted chestnuts or cheap wrist watches.

CHAPTER
EIGHT

The Carriage Trade

Don't ask me how Annie McVey got to our house. She was a big, rosy-faced, cheerful, loud woman about forty-something who had three grown-up children, no husband and stayed in a converted wee shop in Partick. She was the sister of one of my uncles.

I think it was a conspiracy — the second one planned by our well-meaning relatives who seemed always to be pondering the question "What's to be done about the Wilkinsons?" Whatever it was, Annie McVey arrived one evening and told my mother she knew a woman in the West End who had a big house which was let out in apartments to genteel tenants and the woman was looking for a family to be caretakers and do odd jobs in return for the rent-free use of the whole basement. Something like that.

This sort of thing was common in Glasgow — and I expect in other cities too. It was no racket; it was just the way things were and I believe if *our* case was anything to go by, the rent-free tenant got much more out of the deal than the property owner.

Large houses all over the West End of the city had poor families living in the basement rooms. In return for paying no rent they were expected to clean or cook, to keep the gardens right or chauffeur the family car or polish the silver. It was a way for the respective parties to get free accommodation and free service. The system had a boom during the slump years.

I can't believe that my mother and father took the job because we couldn't afford the rent of our own room-and-kitchen house. Maybe. What I *do* believe is that my father thought he would never work again as a shipwright and he and my mother vaguely imagined they could survive economically with no rent to pay as caretakers of a large terrace house in Dowanhill. I also believe, sadly, that they considered me last.

I was ten when we moved. And as I sat on Murphy's coal cart holding our canary in its cage, trying not to cry, I remember watching the little group of my pals waving goodbye before the cart turned into Lyndhurst Gardens. I thought my heart was breaking.

I had never seen 22 Victoria Crescent Road before this day. The coalcart rumbled down the cobbled back lane, behind the grand Victorian terrace, and as I looked around at the grey-black backs of the houses, the deserted, silent, rain-sodden gardens, I felt this was the worst day of my life.

The basement rooms were stone-floored, speckled with cockroaches, and there was a ribbed drain in the middle of the main living room which also housed the boiler and all the gas-fittings. There were iron bars on all the windows and the place stank with damp smells. There was also a pathetic walled garden with sickly grass and tall weeds.

We lived there for three years.

The woman who owned the house was called Miss Jean Wells, a buxom, broad, countrified, cheerful spinster about forty-something. She smoked continuously, wore heavy tweeds and after ten minutes left us to it — she was off to the country.

I can barely remember the people who rented the furnished rooms in that terrace mansion. I knew they were all women, all middle-aged or old and all fugitive from something or other. There were two schoolteacher sisters in the top flat; Miss Petrie, a university lecturer in the second flat; and a cheery old dear called Mrs Yuile on the first floor. The only thing I remember about her was that her daughter at nineteen married a fabulously wealthy man of fifty and they were very happy living down the Clyde coast.

I was not to know it then, but it seems to me now that our début in the West End of Glasgow coincided with the demise of a way of life among the gentry and the well-off in that elegant part of an inelegant city. There was the smell of psychological decay. The old ways were disappearing. Servants were fewer, their uniforms limper, their wages low and their status diminishing.

Shopkeepers in Byres Road, who for generations had served the "carriage" trade, who bustled around loading parcels into m'lady's car and who rubbed hands and "put it all in the monthly account", were being replaced by sharper and blunter butchers and grocers and outfitters who wanted cash on the nail, and no deliveries.

Life was changing for the bowler-hatted, rose-in-the-lapel West End businessman and his afternoon-tea-gowned wife. Nanny holding Robin's little hand while gently pushing the high-wheeled perambulator through Athole Gardens was a rarer sight. The quiet, sun-dappled terraces were slowly but surely being carried in the current towards the mainstream of the uglier city.

I was not to know all this, of course. What those large grey mansions and tree-lined avenues meant to me when I was a boy had something to do with wealth or power and I knew that world was forbidden to me. My place was below stairs in the basement or in the back lane that led to Saltoun Street.

What I do remember with affection were the books the McColl sisters had on the shelves in their room. There were hundreds of them. I think it is odd that two middle-aged schoolteachers should have had as their aptest, most eager, willing pupil a boy of eleven they never met. For that is true — I never once saw the McColl sisters. Our place was "below stairs" and my mother, true to her earlier indoctrination as a maid "in service", warned me never to show myself "up there" to the gentry. To her, all those who did not work with their hands were "gentry".

That first summer when the school closed for the long holiday, I had no friends nearby. The McColl sisters went to their home in the Highlands (Mull, I think), and one afternoon I timidly ventured upstairs. That's when I discovered the books. The sisters' sitting-room was a small library with the three walls shelved and packed with hundreds of volumes of every type under the sun.

I remember beginning with Arthur Mee's *Children's*

Encyclopaedia, then going on to Dickens, then Conan Doyle, Scott, Thackeray and Wilkie Collins. The collection was a pot-pourri of everything, and almost every day I would sit in that sunlit, silent room and devour a menu as mixed as Edgar Wallace and *The Boys' Own Paper Annual* and Arnold Bennett and old copies of the *Strand Magazine*.

That summer was the loneliest and loveliest in my life. Almost every day I would go up to that sunlit room facing the quiet, deserted terrace and read and browse for hours.

My mother didn't know whether to complain to me or not. "Y'know, these aren't *our* books."

"I'm not doing them any harm."

"See you don't mark them or dirty them."

"I'm just reading them."

"You want a cuppa tea?"

"All right. I'll be down in a minute."

It was at the end of that summer I got my first job. I was passing Mrs Foley's newspaper shop in Byres Road when I saw the notice in the window: "Boy Wanted". I walked in and got the job of delivering newspapers early morning and in the late afternoon — five shillings a week plus threepence if I swept the shop out plus threepence if I washed the windows.

The shop was like old Mrs Foley herself — dirty and small. It smelled of old paste, sour milk and cats, and everything seemed a jumble of newspapers, magazines, bottles of ink, school jotters, curled-up writing pads, sun-faded postcards, matches, old-fashioned pens, tatty envelopes, mousetraps, cheap paintbrushes, and worn-out books on shelves that were loaned out for twopence.

Mrs Foley was an old, shrivelled, bleary-eyed woman who wore a horrible old black hat on top of her head each and all the time I ever saw her. I think she slept in it — as well as the black lace jersey and shapeless black skirt she wore. She had one visible tooth that showed when she grinned. I think she was about seventy. She cackled and mumbled and croaked and coughed and shuffled her way from her tenement house on the first floor to the shop below, then back again. When she was in the shop she sat on a stool behind the counter and grinned horribly and servilely at the customers, most of whom were regulars.

She had a son — Dick. He was about fifty, a bachelor, wore spectacles and wheezed. He had a bald head, a pasty face and he *never* came down to the shop before eight-thirty. The two delivery boys — Alf Sweeny and I — sorted out the newspapers with Mrs Foley every morning at five-thirty and we were off on our rounds with them in a big canvas bag by six-fifteen. Alf did the streets and roads on the north side of Byres Road; I did the terraces and crescents and drives on the west. Alf had the apartment-house stairs to climb. I had the surface mileage.

Of course I didn't know why the Foleys had so many customers. For a small, ill-kept little newsagent's shop in Byres Road it seemed to have hundreds of people who bought things or had newspapers delivered.

I think I know now. The Foleys, mother and son,

were among the few shopkeepers who could always be relied upon to keep their place, to nod and smile in subservience and scurry and hurry to fetch the smallest item from the farthest corner of the packed, dusty shelves, who never pressed aloud about an overdue account or an unreturned book from their twopence-a-week library (three shelves opposite the counter). They traded in an age when toadying was being conducted more and more according to the customer's volume of business and his promptness in settling his bills.

It is hard for me today not to be cynical or bitter about those days in the West End of Glasgow. That job with the Foleys taught me some first lessons about human beings — and they were unpleasant ones.

Every other day there would be a complaint from either Mrs Foley or her son that a customer's newspaper was not delivered on time. Whether these complaints were valid or whether it was a trick to get me to deliver more of them I'll never know. All I *do* know is that I walked — sometimes ran — for miles from six-fifteen every morning and got back gasping at seven forty-five, washed the shop window, swept the shop, ran home, got my breakfast, grabbed my schoolbooks, then ran to school two miles away. And I was still failing.

One complaint *was* valid. It came from a big, tall, distinguished-looking man with dark grey hair who caught me on the landing of an apartment building in Richmond Street. He threw open the door of his flat and grabbed his copy of the *Glasgow Herald* before I could put it in his letterbox.

"You're late!"

I mumbled, "I'm sorry —"

"This paper should be here at seven. I've complained twice about it."

"I got — held up, sir."

"I want it here at *seven*." He slammed the door. The time was fifteen minutes past seven.

The gentleman was Glasgow's leading churchman — minister of Glasgow Cathedral.

In all of those months when I delivered the newspapers to the houses of the wealthy, the influential, the notable in the West End of Glasgow, not once from any of these distinguished lawyers and doctors and industrialists and ministers did I receive a gratuity or a token of the slightest recognition — not even a kindly word or greeting. Of course I didn't deserve any word of recognition — what twelve-year-old working-class boy *did* in a city like Glasgow? I didn't smile — life was too earnest. I didn't go out of my way to be pleasant or personable — life was not very pleasant. I don't suppose I was a personable, likeable child.

What I *can* understand today are the circumstances in childhood that can make men and women bitter when they grow up.

People did what they did then far less out of greed or self-interest than to preserve instinctively this thing called a Social Order. When you come to think of it, the upper classes — even in a city like Glasgow — gained very little from their so-called exploitation of the lower orders. The monetary difference between paying five shillings a week and ten shillings a week to a servant for menial duties was *not* the motive. What *was* important to everyone then was that the Order of Things should not be disturbed. A five-shillings messenger boy meant just that. To pay him *ten* shillings was a footstep towards social chaos. And everybody knew it — including most of the five-shillings people. Those who did not or fought it were branded as Bolshies.

I have a notion from my memories and observations of those days in Glasgow that an economic pattern follows a social pattern — not the reverse.

"But what would you do with all that extra money if I paid you it?"

"But that would mean you were getting the same pay as your 'betters'!"

"If I paid you now, you'd *want* more. You'd never know when to stop!"

For this reason, I have the idea that people generally were more content with their lot. We shouldn't forget that the General Strike started with the miners trying to retain their standard of pay — not have it improved.

People generally did not ask for "more". They took what they could get, vaguely estimated where they stood in the social order, and questioned it no more.

I was only once interrogated by a Means Test man. It happened when we stayed in that dank basement flat in Victoria Crescent Road. I was eleven or twelve.

I knew something was wrong when I came into the kitchen and saw the tableau of my father standing at the table with a worried frown on his face, my mother standing at the other side nervously fingering her apron. And, sitting at the table, was a small, bald-headed man wearing a navy-blue raincoat and writing something down on a paper.

I said nothing and waited. After a while the man spoke to my father.

"Only the one child?"

"Yes."

He looked at me. "You're Roddy?"

I nodded. "Yes —" I paused: "sir."

He beckoned me to come nearer. "Come over here, son."

I took a few steps to the table. My mother said, "Just tell the man what he wants to know, son."

The man smiled. "Nothing to worry about, son. You're working? I mean — at the papers?"

I nodded.

"In — where is it? Mrs Foley's shop? Is that the place?"

I nodded.

"What are you paid, Roddy?"

"Five shillings a week."

"And that's all? Nothing else?"

Of course I told him everything — an extra threepence for washing the shop window, another threepence for taking the rubbish to the midden, another for getting the early-morning shopping and another for sweeping the landing and stairway.

"So it's really *six* shillings?" He raised his eyebrows. "Six shillings — is that it?"

I looked at my father and said it was.

The man wrote something on the paper.

After he had gone my parents looked even more

worried and sad. I said, "Did I tell him what he wanted?"

My father sighed. "Aye, ye told him."

I learned a long time later that our unemployment dole money had been cut by a few shillings each week.

CHAPTER
NINE

Jobs Galore

I took on another job about this time. (Well — I finished the evening paper-round at five, didn't I?) It was an old man, Mr Quigley, in a flat in Roxburgh Street who called me into his house one evening.

Mr Quigley wore a velvet smoking jacket and had a cigarette in a holder. He was thin and very straight and lean-faced. His hair and moustaches were white and he walked and talked stiffly.

He lived with two spinster sisters who, like him, were very tall and erect and wore no make-up. All three talked very smoothly and correctly in perfect English without a trace of accent. They were clear-eyed, charming, quiet, eyebrow-raising paragons in my young eyes and I kept wondering if they worked or how they earned their living.

The first time I met Mr Quigley he smiled and invited me to come into his study. Then he sat down in a large red armchair and put his fingertips together.

"Would you like another job?"

"What kind, sir?"

"Oh — just for an hour every evening. All you have to do is get a tramcar down to the city, go to my office, see the manager Mr McNee and fetch my mail. You'll be back well before six."

"All right."

"And you'll get two shillings a week."

"And you'll pay my tram fares?"

"Oh, yes."

It *was* easy. It was also very interesting because Mr McNee, a stoutish, red-faced man, was always doing something peculiar with the typist in the small office every time I called. And he always wore his bowler hat while he was doing it. I thought it very odd.

One evening I called as usual at Mr Quigley's flat. His sister — tall, stately, smiling — opened the door to me and gave me a message. "Mr Quigley's not very well this evening, Roddy. He says you have to ask Mr McNee for the embossing machine and fetch it back here."

Mr McNee pushed his bowler back on his head when I told him. "The embossing machine?"

"Yes."

"*You've* to take it?"

"That's the message."

He looked at the girl, shrugged his shoulders and pointed to the corner. "Help yourself, son."

The machine seemed enormous — and it seemed to weigh a ton. It was a very heavy paper-to-board embossing press.

It took me a long time just to get the machine down the two flights of stairs and along to the tram-stop. I got it on to the tram next to the driver with the help of a man who saw me staggering with it.

Tramcar drivers in Glasgow in those days were lucky

if they could count on a journey from depot to terminus where they had their platform to themselves. Usually they shared it at various stages with tin baths, armchairs, kitchen cabinets, large parcels, a brass-band instrument, a basket of clothing or a tradesman's tool-kit. "Putting it at the front beside the driver" was fair game on the Glasgow tramcars and the driver usually scowled, sighed, asked the destination of the package and put up with the inconvenience for a few miles.

Getting the machine off the tramcar at Byres Road was another matter. I could barely move it from the driver's platform and he was getting impatient. "Get that damn thing off the car! I'm late!" There was a commotion. Two men helped me to get the machine on to the pavement.

Now here is where there was a counterbalance in my young life regarding my impressions of other people.

Watching my struggles with the embossing machine was a young man standing at a third-floor window at the corner of Highburgh Road. His name was Archie Dunlop and he was my officer in the Boys' Brigade at Dowanhill Church.

While I was still trying to lift the machine from the pavement he suddenly appeared over me. He said, "Hello, Roddy. What's that?"

"A printing machine."

"Whose is it?"

"Mr Quigley's. He lives in Roxburgh Street. I've to deliver it to him."

"From where?"

"His office in Bothwell Street."

"He asked you to *carry* it?"

"Oh, no — not all the way. I got it on the tramcar as far as here."

He was tall, broad and strong and he got the machine on to his shoulder and, staggering and tight-lipped, he carried it slowly, solidly and steadily to Byres Road to Mr Quigley's house. His face was shiny as mine had been. He pressed the bell and said to me, "Wait out here, Roddy." He was breathing hard.

It was Mr Quigley himself who opened the door, and he stared at Archie and me.

"Mr Quigley?"

"Yes."

"Did you employ this boy to fetch this machine from your office in town and get it here?"

"Yes, I did. But I —"

"May I come in? I'd like to deliver it to you myself and I'd also like a few words with you."

"Well, yes —"

The door closed and I waited on the landing. Ten minutes later Archie came out grim-faced. He handed me two half-crowns and said, "You're not working for him again, Roddy." That was that.

It was around this time that I discovered the other "caretaker" children. Looking back on it now, the West End of Glasgow must have been coming through the end of one era and the beginning of something else. The servants were disappearing from the big houses — there was no doubt about that. People who inherited large mansions in Beaumont Gate or Athole Gardens didn't quite know what to do with them, because cooks and tablemaids and kitchenmaids and "generals" — all the familiar, starch-aproned regiment of faceless people "below stairs" who were beckoned by bells night and day for years — were now gone. Those who did offer their services (I remember seeing a fading decrepit-looking domestic service agency in Bank Street) wanted fantastic wages, m'dear.

All this brought in the era of the Caretakers — usually a family like ourselves where father was unemployed and could do "odd jobs", mother would maybe do some cleaning or washing and the offspring would learn the virtues of work by making themselves useful. Rent-free. Basement rooms only.

We called her Old Sunshine — the wee, stout, fair-haired woman from Govan who cleaned the rooms upstairs. According to my mother and father she was a Real Card, a Right Old Gossip, a Cheery Wee Wumman and — when they remembered her proper name — Mrs Stoddart.

The rooms she cleaned were those of the paying guests Mrs Yuile, Miss Petrie the university lecturer and the two schoolteacher sisters McColl. As caretakers we were expected to take care of the rest — and that meant my mother doing them.

Old Sunshine *lived* with trouble. It seemed to be part of her cheery, casual nature to have one son in gaol again for "doing" a wee dairy, her eldest daughter pregnant by a coalman, her furniture marked by the sheriff's officer for default in rent and her husband unemployed for six years and drunk every Saturday.

During all the time she came through our basement flat with her ridiculous green hat perched on her head and her arms weighted down with two bags, I never once heard her complain about anything. Yet she talked all the time and picked up all the gossip of the three floors in the house. Somehow she knew that Mrs Yuile was *not* a widow — her husband had left her years before to go to South America. Somehow she picked it up that Miss Petrie was carrying on with a married man up at the university. And how she got to know about the McColl sisters' father's drinking in Tobermory was beyond all credibility.

That was her life — finding out about the "upstairs" people and relating to my goggle-eyed parents the tales of secret tippling, clandestine lovemaking, impoverished backgrounds now veneered with fine talk, stories of debts to bookmakers, family quarrels, ancient disgraces and skeletons in cupboards we never knew about. It kept her going.

The fact that her own room-and-kitchen life in Harmony Row, Govan, was a squalid shambles of unremitting debt, idle, drunken menfolk, sons who were never out of trouble and daughters usually pregnant never seemed to bother her or still her cheerful scandals of the people upstairs. She loved scandal and ignored her own as an alcoholic will talk, talk about the evils of drink before he starts his second bottle of the day.

Old Sunshine used to arrive at our basement kitchen at nine and — still wearing her shabby coat and absurd hat — drink a cup of tea with my mother as she talked, talked. Then she started her work at ten.

I think it was Davie Loudon who got me "in" with the other "caretaker" children. We were the Grey Children, the below-stairs people. We knew our place and never in a million years would we have played around at the front of the houses or anywhere near the enclosed private gardens in the middle of the terraces. Our playground was a happier one — a cobblestoned lane between the walls of our parents' employers, and in the quiet sunlit evenings of summer in the long shadows of the trees and buildings we enjoyed ourselves. I don't think that the "upstairs" people in the big houses knew we existed.

There was no vandalism among us, nor did we thieve, create mischief, deface walls, beat up ourselves or other people. We just played — cricket, rounders, football. We went to the baths at Whiteinch, the Hillhead Saloon cinema in Vinicombe Street, the fish-and-chip shop in a nether area of Partick, and the idea of doing anything bad or bold never entered our heads. We were surrounded by the gardens and terraces of the Establishment.

I only met about half a dozen times the owner of the house in whose basement we lived. Miss Wells was a big, broad, horsey woman with a cheery face and she smoked forty Gold Flake cigarettes a day. My mother and father referred to her as if we were serfs and she the Czarina. To me she was just the woman who came home every few months and sent me to buy more cigarettes when she needed them.

One day when she was home she saw me in the pantry and said: "Roddy, I see there are some nice flowers in the front garden. Who looks after them? Do you?"

"No, Miss Wells, my father does."

"I tell you what I'd like you to do. Will you take a bunch of them to my aunt every Saturday morning? She likes these blue ones. *And* some roses."

"Every Saturday."

"During the summer." She smiled. "Don't worry — she'll reward you."

So I walked the two miles every Saturday to Clevedon Drive at Kelvinside to deliver these flowers to the home of Sir Henry and Lady Wells. I never saw Sir Henry but I *did* see Lady Wells one day. She was a tall, good-looking, dark woman with a pleasant smile and she gave me sixpence for the flowers. After that, Graham the manservant took delivery and paid me each Saturday.

I had good reason to remember this weekly chore three years later.

CHAPTER
TEN

University's for the Gentry

I'll never know to this day whether it was Miss Wells who turned out to be the arch-villain as my father described her or (and this was more likely) my parents messed up their arrangements with her, but what *was* true was that she sold the house and dismissed us.

So here we were again — Dad still unemployed, Mother with no idea where we should go and me at the age of twelve starting to wonder why we didn't have a proper home and stay there for good.

To be fair to her, Miss Wells did talk to a Glasgow house factor who offered us a room-and-kitchen house at Scotstoun West on the main Dumbarton Road. It was a red-sandstone working-class tenement backed by the Clyde and its shipyard cranes and fronted by the tramcars and buses going to and coming from Clydebank. I hated it.

It was now 1931 and there were signs that the Slump was beginning to end. Dad got work in a ship repair yard nearby and we had a regular pay coming in again. I travelled by tramcar to school every day and by this time I was beginning to take an interest in some classroom subjects — particularly English. Now I was feeling the benefit of those long summer afternoons browsing through the library of books in the McColl sisters' room in Victoria Crescent Road.

My mother was ironing one day in the kitchen when I said: "I'll be fifteen next month."

"Ye will that," she said.

"I was thinking."

"What?" She looked up.

"What I should do."

"Oh? Have ye thought about a trade?" She put her hand on her hip. "Yer faither said he'd talk to Tom Pry, the head foreman at the yard. Maybe he could get ye started."

"Started at what?"

"As an apprentice. He was thinkin' o' electrician. Or maybe a mechanic."

I sat down. "Mother, listen. What would be the chances of me thinkin' about the university?"

She stared at me. "What university?"

I shrugged. "Glasgow. Donald Gibson and Jim Slater are thinkin' about it."

"What!" She pursed her lips. "*That's* no' for the likes o' us. We could *never* afford anything like that. That's for them that has fathers in constant jobs, they pay for it."

"Donald Gibson's father's no' rich."

"Get it oot o' yer mind, son. Yer father's just started after *years* o' idleness. No, no." She looked at me decisively. "In fact the quicker you're oot at a job the better. I think ye've had enough schoolin'."

I was angry. "And that's *that*, is it?"

"Aye — that's *that*." She continued ironing noisily and I stumped out of the kitchen.

I was still angry all the following day. That evening after tea, on the way home I got on a tramcar and jumped off at Cleveden Drive, walked up to the big mansion, crunched up the pebbled driveway, and rang the bell.

It was old Graham the manservant who opened the door.

"Hello, Mr Graham. You remember me?"

He lifted his grey eyebrows. "Yes, I do. Roddy, isn't it? My, but you've grown!"

"I used to bring the flowers here every Saturday."

"That's right." He looked puzzled. "Is anything wrong?"

"Could I see Lady Wells?"

He stared, "Now?"

I nodded. "I'd like to ask her something."

"Well, I —" He was holding the door open and behind him in the hall I could see Lady Wells walking down the stairs. She called: "Who is it, Graham?"

"It's — young Roddy. He used to come from Jean's."

"Oh yes, I remember," she said. "How are you, Roddy?"

I gulped. "I — came to ask you if you could help me get a job, Lady Wells."

Graham was wide-eyed. She smiled. "Come in here — into the kitchen."

Lady Wells sat down at the large kitchen table and

watched me, smiling, as I ate the slice of cake and drank the glass of milk she had put in front of me.

"Jobs are very scarce, y'know."

"Yes, I know. But I can leave school now."

"*Now*?"

"On Friday — if I can get a job."

Then I heard a voice from the hallway outside. It was a gruff, growling sound. The kitchen door opened and a short, broad man stood there. He wore no jacket and held a hard white collar with one hand against the neck of his stiff evening dress.

He paid no attention to me and made more growling noises. Her ladyship stood up and said, "Here — let me sort it." She fastened his stud and said, "This is Roddy; you remember him? Brought the flowers from Jean every Saturday."

The little man glared at me and muttered something.

"He wants a job, Henry. At the yard."

More growling and muttering. Then he went out. She sat down and smiled. "You've to call at the office on Monday at eight-thirty. Ask for Mr Stevens."

I beamed. "And I'll get a job?"

"Maybe. I hope so."

I got the job and I left school that week as it was the end of the term. Office boy at eight shillings a week.

It pains me to remember those first few months at work. Very likely I was the worst office boy Wells' ever had. I daydreamed, forgot things, couldn't count or add up correctly, had to be told twice about nearly everything, didn't understand the banter in the office, was teased and reacted badly, didn't mix with other boys, walked home many evenings along South Street with the tears of frustration glistening in my eyes. I was a clunker.

Wells' was a mixter-maxter of a place. Even then it was old-fashioned. The company had grown out of a small back-street factory in Glasgow during the 1914–18 war to this area on Clydeside. They made excellent lifeboats and ship's telegraph gear and — incongruously — lorry chassis frames. It was a very good, hard-working, conservative, stiff-necked, prosperous general marine engineering works. And I was like a fish out of water.

I suppose the Main Office into which I walked timidly that first morning was not much different from dozens of others in shipbuilding yards and factories along the Clyde. There were the high, brass-railed desks with their high backless stools, the large ledgers on shiny old tables, the rolled-up drawings, the cupboards and bookshelves and clickety old-fashioned typewriters. Off the Main Office were the doors of managers and the Head Clerk and the Cashier and — at the very end — the Staff Manager who was also Head Buyer.

The floor was shiny linoleum and the place smelled of old leather and polish.

Outside were the Works. That was where the Men were. There, too, in that strange, noisy world were the bowler-hatted Foremen, the lorries that came and went, the clanging, banging, squealing, thumping world of iron and flames and hammers and shouting.

Beyond that world was the river right down at the foot of the yard where you could look across and see the ships being built on the other side.

* * *

I suppose when you were growing up you had a person who beat you at everything. Sometimes it was an older brother or sister. Usually he was the boy next door whom your mother pointed out to say, "Now why can't you keep yourself as neat and clean as Peter? Just look at him! Never a mark on him."

The Person Who Beats You at Everything is always ahead of you in exams, in sports, with the girls, at getting on with the teacher, getting a good job, and impressing even your own parents.

I met *mine* in Wells'. His name was Jimmy Proudfoot and he was perfect. He was good-looking, tall, modest, worldlywise and clever. Although he was at that time just sixteen — a year older than me — he struck me as one of those horribly handsome young men you see in the women's magazines who pose in knitted cardigans, pipe in mouth, under the headline "For Him".

Everything would have been all right if this paragon had been working at one end of the office and me at the other. The problem was that I was his understudy as an office-boy and was to take over his work, allowing him to be promoted somewhere in the Drawing Office or Accounts or the Purchasing Department.

I could have tolerated him if he had merely been neatly dressed and efficient — which he was. Even if he had been a genius with blueprints or whorl-gaskets or double-entry book-keeping, I could have lived with the situation because my home-made trousers and square-toed Co-operative shoes and converted fourpenny Japanese shirt with no sleeves didn't worry me any more than my inability to keep the postage book in order. But I had two things of which I was very, very proud. I could draw pictures and I could write words. These were the only attributes of any worth I took from school, which, as I say, probably made me the most worthless eight-shillings-a-week liability Wells' had ever employed. The only thing I can say in my defence is that I tried.

I have come to the opinion that nine out of ten people are always behind the times in a career. The tenth person is usually somebody who doesn't give a damn what other people are striving for because he knows they're working on the values of ten years ago anyway.

I first got this idea when I looked back to that first job I got in Wells' as an office boy and I realised that everybody under twenty was there mainly because their father thought it a good thing or because they wanted to follow some timeworn path of ledgers and blueprints and invoices and memos as it was a path they knew or some schoolteacher told them about it. Getting a job in an office on the Clyde was The Thing — it meant security in insecure times.

Of course I couldn't understand all this when I was fifteen. The only thing I felt was being left out of some big secret way of life that made everybody smarter than I was, more intelligent, certainly more acceptable.

All the other office boys — there were five of us altogether — knew everything. Their fathers had told them what was what. They knew all about the postage book and the main ledger and exactly what the Head Cashier wanted on Tuesday mornings and how to answer the telephone. Everything. It was as if I had found myself in a large office of reincarnated people who had all been in this world long before I was born.

"Are you the new boy? Where's Jimmy Proudfoot?"

"That's not the way Jimmy Proudfoot brought me the mail. What a mess!"

"Why don't you do it the way Jimmy Proudfoot did?"

"They should put Jimmy Proudfoot back on your job."

I was sick and tired of being compared to this tall, calm, smiling, good-natured, patient horror who never complained when he showed me for the fourth time that week how to operate the telephone switchboard without cutting the Managing Director off.

One sunny afternoon when we were in the small telephone switchboard room during a lull, we got talking about newspapers and magazines and stories and drawings and the whole world of printed communications. You wouldn't believe it, but he produced from his pocket a "few little things he had done at home" — little pen-and-ink drawings of birds. And they were very, very good. They were far better than anything I could have done. Then he fetched out a few examples of his writing — little poems and short articles and even a short story. They were good too.

He told me that what he really wanted to do was get into advertising or newspapers or publishing — and he knew for a fact that the Staff Manager's sister worked in an advertising agency in Glasgow, and if he played his cards right there might be a vacancy sometime soon.

That was the day I realised I had to get away from that general engineering conglomerate of flanges and cranks and snarling foremen in the tinsmith's shop and vinegar-voiced, aged typists and high desks with brass rails and postage books that never added up and beery-nosed cashiers who wore celluloid cuff-protectors and the whole dreary workaday world of forelock-touching clerks and masses of nondescript workmen who banged hammers all day and swore through broken teeth on their way across to Duffy's Pub in Dumbarton Road or the bookie's shop in South Street.

CHAPTER
ELEVEN

Jazz City

I nearly made it. The *Daily Record* advertised for a copy boy in a peculiar way by running an essay competition. I entered and was invited to call at their Hope Street offices in the city for an interview. When I got off the tramcar at the corner of Bothwell Street I couldn't believe my eyes. There was a long queue of teenage boys which snaked right round the building — hundreds of eager essay-winners. I joined the queue and two hours later didn't get the job.

I got out of Wells' because Jimmy Proudfoot didn't. One day the Staff Manager — a tall, thin, sour-faced man — tapped on the glass partitioning from the main office and signalled to me to go in. I felt awful. I fancied I was about to be lectured, criticised and warned once again about fingermarks on the postage book or screwing up the lines on the telephone switchboard.

"Sit down," he said, and it was then that I saw James Proudfoot, pride of the Clydeside office boys, sitting on the other chair.

The Staff Manager ignored me and went on talking to Jimmy. "Your older brother is in Assam now, is he?"

"Yes, sir."

"Managing a tea plantation?"

"Yes, sir."

"And you'll be going out sometime to join him?"

"Sometime — yes."

He sighed. "That's it, then, isn't it? Any job you take in this country would only be for a few years — is that it?"

Jimmy thought about that. "Yes — I'd think so."

"That's what I felt." He sighed. "All right, James — you can go."

Proudfoot left and I waited for the Staff Manager to give me my lecture on fingermarks in the postage book etc. He looked at me and said,

"I suppose you'd better go."

I half rose, staring at him.

"I believe you're good at that sort of thing," he continued.

I sat down again.

"Writing and art," he said. "That is — if you want to."

"What, sir?"

"Get interviewed for this job at my sister's place."

I gaped.

"It would be no good for Proudfoot. A few years — then he'd be off to Assam. D'you want it?"

"I — er — yes. Yes, I would, sir."

You remember the happy things in your youth, don't you? Those rare little gems of memory that bring back some love and respect for human beings?

I remember the last evening of the last day I worked

in Wells' when I was quite alone in that large office sorting out the last mail for my last delivery to the post office. It was about six o'clock and I thought everyone had gone.

The Managing Director walked along the quiet corridor, bowler-hatted and carrying a small attaché case. He was a glum man, unsmiling, a serious man who always seemed quietly worried. For the past eight months my only connection with this grey-suited, frowning man behind a desk was when I brought in his mail for signing, waited while he bleakly scrawled his signature, "H. E. Moyes", across the letters and silently handed them to me.

This evening he stopped, looked at me and held out his hand to this eight-bob-a-week nobody. "You're leaving us tonight, aren't you?"

"Yes, sir."

We shook hands.

"Well, I'd like you to know something, Roddy. We've appreciated your work while you were here. You've worked hard and late very often and I want to thank you and wish you every success in your future life. Good luck, boy."

I never forgot that man. He was the only person who ever thanked me for anything in that company all the time I was there.

I've never met anybody who was proud of his accomplishments in his early teens. Proud parents, yes. "My goodness, when Peter was fourteen he walked off with all the top prizes at school." Proud of being poor — yes. "When I was fifteen I didn't have a rag to my back. Look at me now." But I've never met anyone who could honestly say, "When I was in my teens I was terrific."

I am no exception. I changed jobs. I didn't change myself. I still daydreamed, did things the wrong way, related wrongly to people and, of course, paid the price in a fairly miserable young working life.

The advertising agency was up three flights of an aged building in Renfield Street and the staff consisted of a bald-headed, tall, good-looking manager called Willie Barnes, a senior assistant called Hugh Campbell, a junior assistant called David Forbes and four women, the oldest of whom was the Wells' Staff Manager's sister. That was the agency. My life was a kaleidoscope of running around the three Glasgow newspaper offices with copy for our clients' advertisements, collecting proofs, checking them, forgetting them, collecting blocks from engravers, dropping them, saying the wrong things and doing most things far too long or too wrong.

Of course I fell foul of many people. The most outstanding of these was a little fat man called Kelly who worked in the advertising department of one of the main daily newspapers in Glasgow. I don't blame *him*. After all, copy delivery at six o'clock at night for insertion in the following morning's edition by a rather dimwitted boy from a small and obscure local agency was hardly likely to encourage him to clear the front page. Moreover he was usually drunk.

One evening I panted into the caseroom of that paper at six-thirty with a late one-inch ad. for the morning paper. He was standing — reeling slightly — at one of the linotype machines and he glared at me bleakly. "What the hell's this?"

"An ad. For tomorrow."

"At *this* time?"

"I'm sorry. We just got the copy half an hour ago."

"You people need a lesson."

We got it the next morning. I'll never know how he managed it, but there was the ad. on the back page beautifully set — upside down.

The client never did better business or got a better response to *any* of his advertisements in his life.

Me? I just got hell.

I was about seventeen when I found Jazz. I was in a pal's house one evening when he put on a record of Duke Ellington's Band playing "Rockin' in Rhythm", then Louis Armstrong's "West End Blues", and that was about that.

Frankly I'm not a good spectator or a good listener. At seventeen I was a terrible audience of anything. I wanted to be *in* the film in the cinema. I didn't appreciate "Hamlet" when I went with the school group to my first play; I would have settled for any part on that stage — even Poor Yorick. You can see people like me at any go-as-you-please talent contest — amateur comedians who never make it and singers to whom the world has far too long been too kind. The amateur stage is filled with people who can neither act nor watch a good play, yet they're *never* in the audience — they're always up there giving a terrible performance year after year and living on the applause of people who haven't the heart to tell them the truth.

In a way, that's how jazz infected me. I wanted to play it. If I had been without dogged perseverance or just got tired or didn't need the money it brought me, I suppose I would have got over it pretty soon. In fact the jazz fever lasted nearly twenty years — and I almost learned how to play it.

Donald Black, the boy who played me those first records, had a drum-kit. He also had a two-row button accordion, which he sold me for ten shillings, which I paid in two instalments. I learned three tunes on this accordion in six weeks: "Springtime in the Rockies", "Whispering" and "Loch Lomond". He had a pal in Govan called Bob Glen who played the black notes on the piano by ear — and we had a band. The only person who played in tune was Donny on the drums.

Bob Glen was the only musician I ever met in my life who had no ear for music yet played with such confident zeal you really thought it was music you were listening to. He played the black notes only on the piano on a percentage basis — about eighty per cent of the notes he hit contributed to the tune and the twenty which did not were struck with such flourishing gusto that he made discords sound as if the composer had planned and scored them that way. And he smiled all the time.

Bob never asked for compliments or criticism because he knew with that superb inner optimism of idiots how good he really was. The way he swung round smiling on the circular stool after an excruciating rendering of "In A Little Spanish Town" defied all description.

His playing of the piano was unbelievably bad but the way his fingers tinkled along the keyboard or struck dominantly on sombre chords, the way he closed his eyes as he played excruciating chords in a soft, sentimental manner — nobody could ever say he had no style.

He was the first — and the last — musical con-man I ever knew.

By the time I had learned a dozen tunes on the accordion and Bob had discovered there were also white notes on the piano, we found we could actually play together if we could be sure of an untuned piano that had the scale of C roughly the same pitch as my scale on the accordion. On such rare occasions, Bob Glen would add variety to the repertoire by placing two pages of the Glasgow *Evening Citizen* between the piano wires and the hammers. The effect was a little like a kazoo player being kicked four-to-the-bar but if you shut your eyes it was just a little like the Grenadier Guards Military Band which, accompanied by my two-button accordion, made something we called "The Sound".

I've often had the feeling that if jazz and blues music had *not* originated in places like New Orleans and if we had had a negro population in Glasgow, then it would have got a tremendous push into the world from our city in the early 'thirties. We seemed to have everything then in Glasgow to make this happen — the Celts from Ireland and the Highlands with sharp ears for rhythmic music, thousands of young people who danced nearly every night, the dogged perseverance of hundreds of young musicians who taught themselves every conceivable instrument from the tenor sax to the mandoline, the environment of Salvation Army bands, Boys' Brigade bands, choirs, and back-street mouth-organ players. Most importantly we had poverty.

It was no accident that many of the big-name dance bands in London at that time who were wildly popular on BBC radio recruited many of their best players from Glasgow. I can think of four musicians I knew who were snatched up immediately.

Glasgow was more than a popular music city. It was a jazz city. And all over the place hundreds of little semi-pro outfits from piano-sax-and-drums to eight-piece bands played to packed dance-halls night after night. I doubt if there was a street or a road that did not have a dance going within earshot.

It didn't take us long to realise that if we were going to make any money from music, two pages of the *Citizen* in the piano and my fixation with the scale of C concert on a leaky two-row button accordion would never achieve it. Somebody had to change. Donny just kept folding his arms over his drum-kit and sucking his teeth. Bob Glen said we couldn't go out looking for engagements on condition that there was a piano in the hall in C concert pitched exactly to my accordion. And, he added, *he* had made *his* contribution — he could now play three tunes on the white notes.

That left me.

I've spoken to many trumpet-players in my time, and when I ask them: "How did you get to playing the trumpet?" they usually smile and say they bought one, took lessons, practised and that was that. Ask me how I came to play the trumpet and I will lead you by the hand back to that Wednesday evening in 1933 when I walked into the church hall at Earlbank Avenue in Scotstoun and sat on a side-seat while twenty-two members of the 122 Company Boys' Brigade Brass Band blasted their way through a Souza march in response to the waving stick of Bandmaster Kerr in his Glengarry Bonnet and well-pressed blue serge suit.

When the band stopped he walked over to me. "Yes, son?"

"I'd like to join, sir."

"The Company?"

"The band."

"Are you in the B.B.?"

"I was. Up in Kelvinside. Then we moved and I left."

"D'you play anything?"

"Just the — No. Nothing."

"Mm."

"I'd like a cornet."

He narrowed his eyes and looked at my mouth. Then he shook his head. "Never. You haven't the lips for it. Got to have fine lips. Small. Narrow. For the triple-tonguing and all that."

"I could learn."

He put his hand on my shoulder. "Give you a euphonium. B Flat. It's a good starter. You want to sit in now?"

In all their lives I never *did* think of thanking my parents for their uncomplaining tolerance in listening to me in our two-room house night after night practising on that thing. Professionally the euphonium is a beautiful instrument. In my hands it was simply a huge, slightly-battered, valve-operated, large-bellied, over-heavy piece of brass plumbing that must have sounded excruciating to my mother and father through in the kitchen. I'll never know how or why they put up with it. Maybe it was because it was a Boys' Brigade instrument.

Nobody showed me how to do anything. And when I sat in with the band I tried to see out of the corner of my eye what valve was being pressed by the other euphonium player. Hopeless. So I went to the public library and made out a request form for a euphonium tutor, got it and started at page one. By the first week I could play a scale. In a month I found out there were other scales and by the autumn I was playing the solo "Asleep in the Deep" accompanied moderato by the band.

It might be hard to believe, but Donny, Bob Glen and I got an engagement. This may have been the very first church-hall dance ever held in the world with a piano-drums-euphonium band. What was certain was that it was the first dance which had a three-piece band of such versatility. Even although we could only play a dozen tunes, the varied combinations of piano-and-Glasgow *Evening Citizen* alternating with my button-accordion and my euphonium were endless. The startled look on the dancers' faces when we struck up at every dance was sensational.

Imagine it. If you had been in that church hall that night you would have heard and seen a drummer, a grinning pianist and me on the button accordion playing "Goodnight, Vienna" as a tango. Then, a few minutes later you would have heard "Blue Moon" being played as if by a small military band slightly out of tune. Naturally, you would have looked up to see me behind a huge brass instrument and, behind me, the pianist playing his instrument with the front taken off and the wires exposed while the hammers banged and twanged on the late edition of that evening's newspaper. You would even have been able to read the headlines if you turned your head sideways.

We got paid with a box of a hundred cigarettes each.

CHAPTER
TWELVE

Petershill Road
Champion Brass Band

It took me five months of oompahs and "Alpine Echoes" but I did eventually get myself out from under the euphonium and behind a cornet. I had every possible attribute for success on this instrument — I could now read music, the bandmaster said my lips were entirely unsuitable, I was mad keen and the idea of me being a musician made my father smile tolerantly because he thought it was ridiculous.

I ran before I could walk. I bought a second-hand mute from a pawn-shop in Partick, got up early every morning, practised scales and exercises, developed an *emboucheur* of sorts, went to work, hurried home, practised more and answered every small ad. in the Glasgow evening newspapers that said "Wanted semi-pro trumpet player for band just forming".

That was how I joined Dougie Henderson's nine-piece Racketeers. I had said goodbye to Donnie Black's trio because the strain of playing on the white notes on the piano became too much for Bob Glen and the trio became a drums-and-black notes duet.

I found the name "Henderson" on the letterbox of a house two flights up a tenement in West Graham Street and Dougie waving his baton in a large bare lounge in front of eight players with real jazz instruments. The noise was deafening.

"I answered your ad."

"You play trumpet?"

"Cornet."

"Mm. Is *that* it?"

"Yes."

"Well — sit in. Take the second trumpet part. We'll hear what it's like."

We played "I'll Never Say Never Again, Again" and "Stormy Weather" and "Over the Rainbow" and "That's a Plenty" and I never felt happier in my life because I could read most of the notes on sight and I seemed to be in tune. There was a pianist, a drummer called Eddie Guliani who had only a small side-drum, a little chap with a string bass, two saxophones and three brass. The trombonist also had a Boys' Brigade instrument. And there was Dougie out in front, tall, good-looking and waving his baton. This was the real thing.

Dougie Henderson was a nice, well-brought-up young man. He was quite tall and he had an aristocratic nose and nice, steady blue eyes. You just couldn't imagine him being anywhere else in a band except out there at the front holding his baton horizontally between two fingers of each hand and smiling goodhumouredly at crowds of dancers. The idea of Dougie with that fine dignified bearing playing a banjo or a string-bass *in* the band was unthinkable. He belonged to another class.

It seemed to be the most natural thing in the world for Dougie to be waving that baton and smiling.

Nobody ever asked him what instrument he *could* play, and I am certain he could play none, couldn't read music and wasn't too sure of the names of the instruments that were in the band.

Nobody seemed to care. He was standing there with his baton and we ignored him. He looked nice and that contented us.

We only did one job. Dougie announced it to us one Saturday after we had mastered five tunes and said he was going to accept it — the annual dance of Glasgow Hibernians F.C. Supporters' Club to be held in the British Limbless Ex-Servicemen's Hall in South Portland Street. The wages — five shillings each plus our tea.

Dougie ran a long and thoughtful meeting in the front sitting-room of his house that Saturday afternoon before we went to the engagement. Should we wear evening dress? (Oh, yes — I had one. I got it for one pound second-hand from a pawnshop in Partick.) Would it be fitting? No? Well, perhaps not. After all, it *was* a football supporters' club dance. Were we all quite sure how to get there? Did we have our scores? Should we have one more rehearsal?

That dance wasn't an engagement — it was a nightmare. I suppose it all started because Eddie Guliani didn't have a drum-kit. So we borrowed a bass drum from a Salvation Army hall in Govan. The drum was enormous. It was the biggest carry-all-before-you bang-up drum I had ever seen. Around the skin were the words "Number Fourteen Tent, Govan Salvation

115

Army", and the rim of the drum had large holes cut in it the size of soup plates so that the drummer in front of the band could look through them and see which way he was going. Very practical.

The whole kit — big drum, side-drum, Chinese cymbals, foot-pedal and sticks — was precariously held together by an all-embracing bed-tick sack for portage.

The dance *started* all right with "I'll Never Say Never Again, Again". The Master of Ceremonies was a short, squat, fresh-faced man with baby-pink complexion and the clear-blue eyes of a born killer. The more he drank, the more he asked for outlandish dances like the Embassy Tango, The Circassian Circle and the Pride o'Erin Waltz. Our repertoire was exhausted in twenty minutes and we were reduced to the only piece we could be sure of playing by ear together with any cohesion — "Whispering" in E Flat. The trouble was that we played it for a slow foxtrot, tango, rumba, St Bernard's Waltz and a Military Two-Step.

It was that two-step that did it. The MC by this time was flushed-drunk and the dancers were ugly. I remember us packing up our instruments in a vulgar hurry and scurrying through the rear kitchen to the back lane to escape — all except Eddie Guliani whose kit-packed bed-tick got stuck in the doorway. Dougie — brave soul — ran back and extricated him before six of the hard men got to him.

I didn't stop running till I caught a tramcar going over Broomielaw Bridge to my home.

* * *

Mr McManus was a wee, squat, timid man who rang our doorbell one Thursday evening just as I was getting myself changed into evening dress to play at a dance in Partick Burgh Halls.

My mother brought him into the bedroom. "There's a Mr McManus to see you, son."

I was sorting out my clip-on black bow tie. "Hello."

He held his hat in his hand as my mother closed the door behind him. "It was Sam Collins who said I should come and see you."

"Oh, yes. What was it about?" I put on my black jacket.

"I'm the captain of the 186 Company Boys' Brigade."

I stared at him. "Boys' Brigade?"

"Yes. And it's about our brass band." He smiled cautiously. "We don't have a bandmaster." He fumbled with his hat. "And Sam Collins thought that maybe you would have the time to look after the lads until we can get one."

"Look after them?"

"Yes — you know — keep them together. We don't have anybody. And they keep turning up with their instruments twice a week and there's just nobody to lead them or show them what to do."

I hesitated and I was lost. I asked, "Where's the place?"

He sat down. "Petershill Road, Springburn. It's that big church at the corner." Now he was speaking faster. "And we've got all the instruments and music and everything. And it won't be long till we *get* a bandmaster. If you could just keep them playing somehow for a few weeks . . ."

I took it on — Tuesdays and Thursdays only on condition that I was not playing my trumpet at an engagement anywhere else on these nights.

The band was pathetic. When I went into the bleak church hall that first Tuesday there was a full turnout of fourteen boys holding leaking trombones, horns with stuck valves, cornets with bashes all round the tubing, a double-bass with a hole at the base and two euphoniums that had the wrong type of mouthpiece. The boys were between eleven and fourteen years of age, ill-dressed, some unwashed and all of them desperate for somebody to tell them what to do.

I sighed and got to work.

"Put your hand up anybody whose instrument doesn't play at all."

Two hands went up.

"Let me hear."

Nothing. No sound.

It started like that. The company *had* some funds so we got some vital repairs done to the worst mauled of the instruments and we were off.

Off where? Well, I don't remember too much about those dreary dark nights when I changed to three tramcars to get up to that grey church hall in Springburn; when I showed those fourteen boys which valve to press, which trombone slide position to adopt, which way to blow in order to follow crotchets and quavers on sheets of music they barely understood. Nor do I remember too much about that first glorious night we actually played a tune *in tune* together.

What I *do* remember is a girl called Mae Ritchie

whose father was a fireman in Whiteinch and who accepted my invitation to come and listen to the band's very first concert in Townhead Hall (collection in aid of the United Mission — two sausage rolls with a cup of tea included).

The band played two simple marches by Souza, a one-two-three easy Austrian waltz, three hymns and God Save the King. Mercifully there was also a display of acrobatics by the Life Boys and a short play by the Girl Guides.

I never could understand why I only saw Mae twice after that. I thought that perhaps she didn't like brass-band music.

I can never be too sure how or why I got so many Jewish friends in Glasgow during my days of playing the trumpet. They were musicians, of course, and like me had taught themselves saxophones and pianos and trombones and string-basses, to play night after night for an honest copper. One way or another I found myself "in" with the Jewish people around South Portland Street and Oxford Street south of the river.

I stress the fact that they were Jewish because Solly Wolfson and Maxie Ross and Maurice Levy and the others were not spare-time jazz musicians who happened to belong to the Jewish faith; they were up to their necks in everything we had come to associate with Scottish Jewish people. Their fathers built little clothing or furniture businesses with their bare hands from nothing; their mothers were always smiling and cooking marvellous Yiddish food; all of them belonged to the Jewish Institute where I played every Friday night; and during that period I seemed to be eating more unleavened bread and wearing a hat at table than at any other time in my life.

Then the movement started. Solly Wolfson's family moved first to Clarkston, then to a bigger house further south to Whitecraigs. There seemed to be a gradual migration then, and by the time the war started all my friends had moved from the Gorbals tenements to nice houses with gardens.

My fondest memories were of those large, dark, sprawling tenement flats around Norfolk Street, the smell of Jewish food cooking and everybody talking at once.

Not so many things were syndicated or multiplied or mass-produced in Britain in the 'thirties. Of course, there were the newspapers, the goods in the shops, the ready-to-wear suits. But there was a lot left for the one-off people. That is why hundreds of small bands could get one-night jobs — there were no discos. Stage comedians could go on tour with the same material for years — there was no television to kill the jokes after one show. Showcards and posters in many shop windows were supplied by back-street ticket-writers galore — there was no silkscreen printing. Slump or no slump, however, they were wasteful days. I have noticed this about economic depressions — it has always seemed to me that the more people don't have, the more they will waste or throw away.

It was one Friday evening about five o'clock in 1933 that I went into our poster and display studio where the company employed about twenty men painting cinema posters and display cards. The head poster-writer was a small, thin man called Hank who spoke with an American accent, mainly, I believe, because he had worked for a year in New York and on his return to Glasgow adopted the name and the twang. It gave him distinction.

"What're you doing, Hank?"

"Cleanin' out the paint dishes."

I watched him dislodge the hardened poster-paint from the little ceramic dishes and throw them into a waste-bin. "What's wrong with it?"

"Nothin'. But I don't use hard paint Monday mornins. Always use fresh — right out of the jar."

"What's the matter with hard paint?"

"Takes a helluva time to soften up again with water."

"Can I have them?"

"Sure. Help yourself."

I got a book out of the library that night and I got six of my mother's empty jam-jars and I used hot water and a twopenny bottle of gum — and I had six beautiful jars of restored poster paints in vivid colours. I bought a square-headed ticket-writer's brush and I was in business. All I needed was some blank cards. Oh — I also needed to know how to letter.

I loved — and still love — city libraries. In Glasgow in the 'thirties they magnetised me because I found you could learn almost anything about anything in them. I was hooked on them.

I discovered something else, too, that has stood by me all my life. Librarians are lovely people. They are quiet, solemn, bookish people who are simply *dying* to show somebody their expertise in knowing exactly where to find the original version of Ballantyne's Law of Interbalanced Isotopes. Yet what happens? People shove their returned books at them over a counter and the librarians scurry through thousands of tickets to find theirs. Then they go to a counter on the other side and thump a rubber stamp on outgoing books. Their scholarly souls are strangled.

So I found out the best way of learning about any subject. I didn't plough my way through massive catalogues or card indices. I simply asked the tweed-skirted, bespectacled lady with the woollen twin-set and she found me exactly the book I wanted.

I got blank cards from offcuts in the studio waste-bin and I learned how to letter by brush by watching Hank and practising at home for hours and hours — sometimes by candlelight in my room so that my mother wouldn't know I was still working.

Getting the business was easy. Each evening after work I walked the five miles home along Argyle Street and Dumbarton Road calling at all the little cafés ("Hot peas twopence a plate"), the hairdressers that were still open ("Shave and haircut fourpence"), the fish-and-chip shops ("Sausage and chips fivepence"). Then I would hurry through my tea at home and do the cards and posters. The following evening I delivered them and collected the money. I charged about two shillings a card.

It was when I began calling on the drapery shops and even some of the smaller department stores along Partick and Whiteinch that I began to get into the Big

Time with sales bills and price tickets and cut-out fancy cards and Christmas posters. And so I was now earning from this freelance business twice what I earned in my daily work.

CHAPTER
THIRTEEN

The End of the Holiday

The tramcar time from our home in Scotstoun to the centre of Glasgow was about half-an-hour. And it was during that time I began writing short stories. I bought myself a second-hand typewriter and after finishing the showcards at home I would start work typing my stories.

I was sixteen when I sold my first one.

They tell me no writer ever has a greater thrill in his life than when he sees his first piece in print. It was my father who found mine on page five of the *Sunday Mail* one Sunday morning at nine-thirty when we were having breakfast round the kitchen table.

"I see there's a story in the paper here written by somebody same name as yourself."

I stared at him. "Where?"

He held up the paper to show the half-page story horribly illustrated.

I nearly tore it from his hands. "That's *my* story!" My mother shouted, *"Your* story?"

"Yes."

"You wrote it?"

"Yes."

Everybody was beaming, arm-thumping, back-slapping. I never saw my parents look so incredulous or happy.

During my lunch-hour the following day I hurried breathless to the offices of the *Sunday Mail* in Hope Street, asked to see the editor, told the commissionaire at the front counter who I was, saw him telephone somebody upstairs and was told to go to Room 68 and Mr Foster would see me.

He was a lean-faced, dark-eyed man in a tweedy suit and when I went into his office he said: "You wanted to see me?"

"Yes, Mr Foster. I'm Roderick Wilkinson."

"Are you?"

"Yes. And — well, I just wanted to call and thank you for printing that story of mine yesterday."

"Did you?"

"Yes. I'm glad you liked it."

"Are you?"

Silence. I had nothing more I thought I could say.

At long last he said: "You've probably written more of them."

I smiled. "Yes, I have. In fact I have another two here . . ."

"Are they like the one we published?"

"Well, no — they're different. But they're just as good."

He rose and sighed. "Listen, young man, I have no wish to dampen your zeal but I think I should tell you something about that story of yours. On Friday night

I was told in a hurry by the editor to fill half a page with a story or a feature. I looked through our files and found my secretary had returned to their authors every story we had — all except one." He paused.

"Mine?"

"Correct. Yours. So we published it." He frowned.

"You — liked it?"

"No, I didn't. Neither did the editor. In fact if you want to know the truth, it's one of the tripiest stories we've ever published. It has no decent plot or characters. Oh, we'll pay for it — don't worry. But I want to save you time and postage if you're thinking of sending us any more like it."

I walked back to the office up Renfield Street feeling furious, chastened, desperate and mainly scared because I knew he had told me the truth. That week I wrote and wrote and wrote. Within the next six months I had sold about a score of articles and stories to the weekly magazines and newspapers. *And* I sold another one to the *Sunday Mail*.

Naturally, I collapsed. I got up one morning, washed, came through to the kitchen to have breakfast, perspired, and fell flat on my face. My mother got me on to the armchair, ran down for the doctor (a man we had never even seen before) and after he had examined me thoroughly, he straightened up and said to my mother: "Getting all his sleep, is he?"

"No, he isn't. Busy at everything — just everything. Playin' in bands an' doin' these shop posters an' writin' stories on tramcars. Never stops."

"Mm. He'd be far better with a regular, steady job."

She stared at him. "But he's got one."

"As *well*?"

"Yes."

He pursed his lips. "He's played out. Keep him off work for a week." He wrote a prescription. "Give him these tablets three times daily and make sure he gets plenty of sleep. Growing lad. Doing far too much."

I went back to work next day.

Life in the advertising agency was like a small rat-race on a small circuit. The boss was fired by the owner in London and Hugh Campbell took over the place in Glasgow. David Forbes and I got ourselves promoted to sharing a small room together and life went on with the press advertisements, posters and front-of-house showcards for cinemas, theatres, ice rinks and dance halls. We were neither skilled nor willing to tackle any other kind of advertising — we left that to the "respectable" agencies in town and we never met any of their people because we were too busy, too "amateur" and generally too poor. In any case I don't think any of us would have known how to produce good visual ideas, copy and artwork to please the more sophisticated whisky, food and engineering clients so miserly guarded for years by those other agencies. We didn't know the "language", didn't have the skills or even the initiative to enter that arena. So we stuck to what we knew. And, in an odd way, the place progressed. At least it made money.

There were four rooms plus a tiny reception lobby in that agency. And, frankly, it looked not much different from hundreds of other little businesses all over Glasgow — small insurance offices or textile agencies or two-men-and-a-girl accountants.

What seemed normal and quite acceptable then seems so silly today. If a visitor came into the small reception lobby, he pressed a bell. I would be immediately behind a partition which had a sliding window which I opened to ask him his business. Really it would have been easier and quicker for me simply to open my door and see him or even for me to stand on a chair and talk to him over the top of the partition. But the sliding window was the thing — not only in our minuscule office but throughout the world of small Glasgow businesses. I think the idea came from medieval times and the spyholes in castle walls.

I met the owner from London — a short, silent, squat, grim-faced Scot — only twice, and as he walked through our silly-looking little four-room office I nearly genuflected.

It was about 1937 when life began to change for the better in our house. My father got work in a ship-repair dockyard near our house (as a matter of fact it was just behind the house on the riverside), and for the first time in years we didn't seem to have serious money troubles. My mother began buying things like carpets and chairs and — wonders! — a brand-new radio.

In any case, by this time I was standing on my own feet. Between my earnings from the spare-time showcards business, the spare-time dance band business (I was playing every night) and the full-time work in the agency, I could buy my own clothes, pay my own tram-fares, smoke my own cigarettes, buy my own books and still put pound notes into the tea-caddy on the mantelpiece every Friday to help keep the house going.

In the early 'thirties it was possible to get a two-week camping holiday on the Isle of Arran for about two pounds. The man who put this idea to me was called Paddy McKee, the wee unemployed riveter from Partick who had a wee wife and six children. He said to me one day in our house: "D'ye have a tent?"

"No, but my pal Andy Russell has."

"Right. Well, ye get that tent an' all yer stuff intae a big boax or a hamper an' get it doon tae the Broomielaw and oan the Campbeltown boat that stops at Lochranza an' if ye write tae the farmer at Catacol he'll pick ye up at the pier wi' yer boax an' let ye camp on his wee paddock just up from the shore for two-an'-a-tanner a week an' that's you for the fortnight. Great. Yer fare on the boat's about five bob."

And that's what we did, Andy and me, when we were about seventeen. It was great fun. Wee Paddy McKee had been doing this with his family for two weeks every summer with a huge ex-army bell tent for years.

I don't know where or when my father got to know wee Paddy McKee — probably in the dole queue — but he was the best tonic he'd ever had. Unemployment with Paddy was endemic; he'd been on the dole for years and, unlike people like my father who worried about it year in year out, he came to terms with it. So he decided the dole was his fate and — far from giving up normal living — he enjoyed life to the full. He was dole-happy, benefit-happy, family-happy — just happy about everything. Getting his legitimate rights from the authorities was his main occupation, his relations with his six children were his pride, his hobbies were getting books from the library on subjects like walking, home-made lemonade, shoe-repairing and hairdressing — anything that would get more from less.

As an undersized shipyard riveter he just laughed hysterically at the idea of getting work ever again. He didn't drink, had no connections with foremen, was so far behind in his dues to his union that, as he put it, "A thoosand pounds wid jist get me cards back!"

What he did for my father was simple — he convinced him that life is here to be enjoyed as best we can, dole or not, work or not, money or none. He was the cheeriest, poorest little soldier I had ever seen in that long war of poverty in Glasgow.

Camping and hiking and cycling from Glasgow in the slump years were, if not invented, certainly traditionalised by the unemployed. All along Loch Lomondside, for instance, groups of mouth-organ-playing, ukulele-twanging, singing campers from the back streets of Glasgow set up a lifestyle that still has rough echoes today. Whole families would spend every weekend "drumming up" with little Primus stoves either under canvas or in the rock caves of the wild, beautiful places in the West Highlands. Getting out into the open air from the foetid, tramcar-clanging atmosphere of a depressed, workless city was the aim of thousands of young people who either cycled or simply walked from the bus terminus they could afford to reach.

I know at least half-a-dozen settled, successful men

today — including one world-famous naturalist and photographer — who got their first taste for the rivers and mountains of the Scottish Highlands in those dark days when thousands of the unemployed migrated from Glasgow every Friday evening in summer.

I was twenty-two when I took what ordinary people might call an ordinary holiday. Andy Russell, Andy Baillie and I went to the Isle of Man for a week in September — to Cunningham's Holiday Camp. I had never seen a large coastal holiday resort before and I just couldn't believe that this "other world" had existed for years. I thought Glasgow was the world.

It was on the way home we got the news.

I was lying on my back on the steamship listening to the radio. Suddenly there was a pause in the programme and a voice said: "Here is the Prime Minister." Then we heard Neville Chamberlain utter those historic words in a deep, solemn voice. Everyone in the cabin listened silently and when he had finished, Andy Russell leaned his head over from his bunk to mine and said, "I think that's the holiday over."

I said, "Yes — for everybody."

When we disembarked at Stranraer and got on the train there were strange-looking, sausage-shaped barrage balloons dangling all over the place.

My mother was crying when I got home.

CHAPTER
FOURTEEN

Joining Up

I joined up in the army in a funny kind of way.

At one time, they said, he'd been the crack-shot of the British army in India — and I could well believe it as I sat opposite Sergeant-Major Wright at tea that Saturday evening in my uncle's house in Coatbridge.

"Well, it's started now, alright," said my Uncle Jim as he passed the pan-loaf bread.

"Terrible, isn't it!" My aunt sighed.

"Bound to start sometime," growled the Sergeant-Major. "Bound to. Been brewing for months."

I cut my ham on the plate. "You're stationed quite near here, are you?"

"Over there —" He nodded over his shoulder. "RAOC's a new unit. Getting it together."

My uncle explained. "It was a territorial unit. Now it's mobilised."

Then, as if he had just seen me for the first time, the Sergeant-Major laid down his knife and fork. "You're not in one of them reserved jobs, are you?"

I stared. "Reserved? No, I don't think so."

"Time you were in, lad!"

"In where?"

"Army."

I looked at my aunt and uncle. They coughed and carried on eating.

"What're you waiting on, then?" said the S.M.

I shrugged. "I don't know. War's only been on three days."

"Think it over, boy," he almost orated. "Best place in the world to be at this time. Get yourself round there an' take the King's Shilling." He sounded like a recruiting sergeant from the Peninsular War.

Well, I *did* think it over. It seemed to me a clear alternative to waiting around for conscription papers and the fell hand of authority yanking me off somewhere whether I liked it or not.

"What do you *do*?" asked the sergeant at the counter.

"I'm in advertising."

He stared at me. "What the hell are you doing here?"

"Sergeant-Major Wright said I could join up here."

"Where did you see him?"

"At my aunt and uncle's house in Coatbridge. He was having tea with them last Wednesday and said it was high time I was in uniform and I may as well enlist into his unit here."

"You know what this is — the RAOC workshops."

"I know. You're engineers."

He sighed. "Well — all right. We'll take you. Fill in that form." He looked at the ceiling in disgust. "Advertising! Phew!"

I was a soldier in three days.

I had no notion about engineering — in or out of the army. Engines, gaskets and crankshafts bored me. The world had always seemed to me to have too many engineers, anyway — most of them unemployed. The only reason I joined this small unit of the Royal Army Ordnance Corps was because I wanted to get into the war as quickly as possible and I hated the idea of waiting for months to be conscripted. The sooner the better, I thought, and one army unit was as good as any other.

The unit was situated in a small disused ironworks in the middle of an out-of-the-way industrial area of Coatbridge. There were about a hundred soldiers billeted in the place when I enlisted and Fred Carno would have signed on the lot for his circus if he had seen us on parade, half of us wearing civilian overcoats (the army coats hadn't come through) and the other half with no rifles. ("Don't worry, sonny boy — you'll get one on Saturday.")

Life in that unit as I remember it during those first few weeks was a motley of young, cursing, swearing, small-town lads vaunting their new-found soldierly manliness and flexing muscles they didn't have. In a way, they were like children who suddenly found themselves with no parents or nannies or schoolteachers around — so they raised hell and pretended they knew all about the army.

I was miserable. Morning after morning we lined up in the early winter frost to be sorted into groups for road-mending and window-washing and potato-peeling and ditch-digging and floor-washing. All the NCOs and mine host Sergeant-Major Wright pretended they had been in the army for centuries and knew everything from grenade-throwing to driving a tank. If there had been live ammo. in that place they would have blown it up.

One morning I lined up as usual in the yard and the Corporal called off the working parties as usual. "You, you and you on the road job. This six over here on the ditches. This six here washing the floors." Then he looked at me. "You're in the Sergeants' Mess."

I thought, "Great! I've been made a Sergeant."

I was in the Mess, all right — as an orderly. I had to clean it, get the food for the three-stripe inmates, serve it, wash the dishes, get coke for the stove and do just about everything any sergeant thought about.

One morning I heard through the Mess window the roar of motorcycles coming and going. The noise went on all morning and I walked round to where there was a group of soldiers in crash helmets and goggles, some mounted on brand-new motorcycles.

"What's going on?" I asked one of them.

"Despatch riders."

"What despatch riders?"

"Us. Getting taught how to ride them."

I fetched my AB64 Pay Book out of my pocket and looked at it. It said, "7616715 Wilkinson Driver I.C. (DR)."

"What's Driver I.C. (DR)?"

"Despatch rider."

I went up to the Sergeant. "I'm supposed to be a Despatch Rider."

He glared at me. "Who says?"

"It says it in my Pay Book."

He looked at it. "Where the hell have you been? We've been at it all morning."

He didn't seem to remember who had been serving him his meals in the Mess for a week.

"Can I start now?"

"You've missed *hours* of it. Here — take this crash helmet and get on."

I mounted a motorcycle for the first time in my life. The Sergeant kick-started the machine and over the roar of the engine I heard only three things — something about kicking the gear-change, raising the hand-clutch when I did so and the twist-grip throttle. The bike went off with me aboard and I hadn't the faintest notion how to stop it. I got on to the main road, kicked something desperately on the machine in conjunction with the hand-clutch — and I was now going nine times faster along Canal Road, round Coatbridge Cross and up Corswell Street with no idea in the world how I got the thing stopped.

I stopped it all right — smack into the sloping back of the adjutant's car.

When I was lying in the little military emergency hospital round at Blairbeth Road a pal of mine, John Symington, came to see me.

"I can understand why *your* name's on the list of volunteers but not mine."

I sat up and drew my bruised leg over the bed. "What list? Volunteers for what?"

"Orkney and Shetland Defences."

"*My* name?"

"That's right. We move out on Wednesday — fifteen of us."

We did.

The story — as I've since read about OSDEF — ran something like this. The Germans sank the *Royal Oak* in Scapa Flow. A U-boat sneaked in on a rising tide through a passage between the islands called St Mary's Holm, put two torpedoes into the warship, then slipped out again before the tide turned.

I like to think it was Winston Churchill who said, "Get that damn Scapa Flow place defended — it's Britain's soft upper-belly." Anyway, they formed a thing called the "R" Plan with AA gun emplacements and naval guns placed all around the Orkney Islands in the shape of the letter "R". Then that was scrapped in favour of the "Q" Plan, which stuck. War Office gave orders to Major-Generals who gave orders to Brigadiers who instructed Colonels who ordered Majors to assign Captains who ordered Lieutenants to get fifteen volunteers from the Divisional Workshop Company RAOC in Coatbridge. And I was one of the fifteen.

Everything went wrong. All our kitbags were sent to the Faroe Islands by mistake so we had nothing but our rifles and what was in our side-kit. The journey was terrible. It took us three days to get to Stromness and the snow was feet deep. We had no food, pay, cutlery, ammo, medical supplies or soap or towels or razors.

Stromness was like a small white Arctic port swarming like flies with thousands of soldiers, trucks and small navy boats. Nobody seemed to know who was leading what where, or why.

We got our billet all right — it was an old disused distillery at the north end of the town — and if we thought *our* luck was bad, all we had to do to cheer up was listen to the men in the Royal Engineers Company who had been staying in the place since the war started in September.

The nearest picture to the one I saw that night when we dragged ourselves into that rat-infested place was of the Bastille in the film, "A Tale of Two Cities". There were dozens of double-tier wooden bunks all over the main distillery and eight of these were allocated to us. The place was lit by oil pump-lamps that gave out a greeny-white glare. Men were sitting around playing cards and crown-and-anchor and one bearded chap with a husky voice told me they usually played all night because they couldn't sleep anyway because of the cold. He offered me a swig from his bottle of navy rum; it looked as thick as varnish.

We filled our palliasses with straw from the backyard, drew three blankets each from their store and hunted for something to eat. There were rumours every five minutes that there was a cook somewhere, that they were trying to dig out some "iron rations", that one of our own lads had discovered a kitchen at the back.

I said to John Symington, "Got any money?"

"Ten bob."

"Maybe there's a chippy or something in the town."

We went out into the snow and crunched along the narrow white streets of Stromness. After half a mile I saw a figure standing at the corner of one of the little harbours — a policeman.

"There's a bobby," I said. "Let's ask him."

He was a tall, broad, mild, slow-speaking Orcadian with high cheekbones. "A cheepy?"

"Yes — a fish 'n chip shop. Or something?"

He smiled. "Is it something to eat you'll be wanting?"

"That's right."

"The place you're wanting's up here." He led the way up a steep hill towards a snow-covered building like a church. "I'll take you in."

It was a Mission Hall — warm, steaming from the tea-urns, packed with soldiers and aproned women, noisy and unbelievably welcome. I began to wonder if they'd let us take our palliasses and bed down here after they closed.

The policeman's name was Bob Wylie and he took us right over to a large, stout, cheerful woman who was his wife. "Here's another two, Agnes."

She looked at us, smiling. "Are ye just here?"

I nodded. "Yes — today."

She looked around at the trays of scones and cakes and biscuits. "Have ye *had* a meal?"

"Yes," I said. "Yesterday — at Thurso."

She raised her eyes to the ceiling. Then she poured two mugs of tea, put them in our hands with a large scone each and said, "Ye'd better have that just now. I'll be finished here in a wee while and I'll tak' ye round to the house for something to eat. Sit down over there."

We sat down and finished the tea and scones and waited. P.C. Wylie went out.

I said, "This is The Place."

"You're right."

"I'm bedding down here."

"Don't be daft — you'll be court-martialled."

"Anything's better than that hell-hole of a distillery."

Before we left to go round to the Wylie house I looked over my shoulder and saw a man switch off the lights of the Mission Hall and close and lock the main doors with a noisy key. That was that.

Nothing very exciting happened to our family during the Clydebank Blitz. Yes, our tenement house *was* by the Clyde and right in the target area.

Yes, the air raid *did* last for two nights. Yes, thousands of people *were* killed and injured. But — as usual — we only had confusion, emotion, fear, and were homeless again. Typical.

Actually, I was three hundred miles away when it happened. A corporal burst into our Nissen hut in Stromness and said, "They've knocked the hell out of Clydeside."

"Who?"

"Germans. Two nights of blitz. All down Clydebank flattened. They're bringin' the dead out in thousands."

Before he got to the word "thousands" I was running across to the adjutant's hut to ask for compassionate leave. I got it.

Before I packed my kitbag I tried to get through on the telephone from our Orderly Room to the REHQ in Kirkwall, who tried to get through to REHQ in Glasgow. There was no reply; all lines were down.

From Glasgow Central Station I got a tramcar as far

as Scotstoun West and I walked the rest of the way along Dumbarton Road, which was littered with broken glass and pieces of wood and bricks and all sorts of things. The red sandstone tenement building which had my home on the top floor of Number 2037 was still standing and there seemed nothing wrong with it. The docks behind the back-court looked as grim and horrible as usual; the closes were still there — empty and lonely. There were no people around. It was like a graveyard.

I went up the stairs and saw the first damage — a gaping square hole where the stairhead window should have been. The stair was full of powdered glass and I crunched my way up to the first landing.

The door of the McVeys' house was hanging by one hinge. On the next landing all the doors were intact but the stairhead window was, again, lying in powder form around the stairs.

Then I got to *our* landing — the top floor. The door was locked but I had my key and I opened it.

"Hello."

Silence.

I went into the kitchen. The wind was blowing in through the glassless window. It was the same in the room and my feet crunched and crunched over powdered glass.

Everything else seemed to be there and intact — wardrobe, dresser, table, chairs. Some things were gone. I opened the wardrobe and found no clothes. There was no china, cutlery, towels or soap.

I sat down with my rifle and kitbag leaning on the dresser.

"Where have they gone?" I asked.

Back came the possibilities. Killed? Taken to hospital? Missing presumed dead?

I jumped up, opened the door and went out to the landing. I knocked on the door next to ours — it belonged to old Mr and Mrs McDonald, the Highland couple. No answer. I tried the opposite door — the Christies. No answer.

Then I heard a door opening downstairs on the second landing and up came Mrs Anderson's voice, "Is that you, Roddy?"

"Yes, Mrs Anderson."

"Are ye looking for yer faither and mother?"

"Yes — where are they?"

"They ran away, son."

I walked down the stairs. "Ran away where?"

She looked at me anxiously. "Night before last — well, first thing in the morning. They packed a few things in a suitcase and ran."

"Where did they go?"

"Nae idea, son. What a coupla nights!"

"Yes, I heard about it."

"Clydebank's got the worst of it. They say there are thousands dead."

"Was it bad?"

"Terrible. Bombs an' land-mines an' incendiaries a' night long. Then they came back the next night an' it was worse. We were jist on the edge of it."

"I see the building's not damaged."

"Naw, but maist of the windows are oot."

"I'd better go on the hunt for them."

142

"Aye. They'll be somewhere. Yer mother was in an awful state — awful!"

I tried Whiteinch School. That was where they were keeping records of the dead and injured — and the missing. A big ARP man in blue uniform and dark-blue steel helmet said, "We've no record here of them. Maybe they've gone to some relative."

They had. I found them in Coatbridge in Aunt Marian's house in Corswell Street. They were wide-eyed, frightened, excited, glad to see me and as usual all love and disorganisation. Aunt Marian wasn't quite sure how long they would stay or why they came or when they might go back home. But she was kind enough — certainly to me.

CHAPTER
FIFTEEN

Soldiering

When I got back to Orkney, I realised that unless I did something about it, I might be there until the end of the war. I have an idea that this is what the army did with soldiers who did nothing very heroic or criminal or noble or disreputable. They just let them stay where they were last posted because they were not very important one way or another.

I decided that this was what was happening to me. So I complained and said I wanted a posting — somewhere.

It took weeks and finger-drumming and chin-pulling and hemming and hawing with grunts and sighs, but in the end I got what I wanted — a move to another unit. It turned out to be a group of REME workshops in the Tyneside area. Well, it was something.

It was around this time that I began to wonder why on earth I was in the Royal Electrical and Mechanical Engineers at all. As I told them when I enlisted in Coatbridge, I couldn't mend a fuse, fix a puncture, replace a tap washer or understand how an alarm clock worked. Why they took me in when they could have had the pick of thousands of motor mechanics, fitters, plumbers, electricians, maintenance men and truck drivers is still beyond me. Perhaps I should have told them about that manual teacher at school who actually hit me in uncontrollable frustration at my sixth attempt at making a teapot stand for my mother.

Yet there it was. I was in REME. While I was at Stromness, I remember a memo sent to my commanding officer from Records Office in Leicester saying that 7616715 Wilkinson since the date of his crash-up with a motor cycle in Coatbridge would no longer be registered as a Despatch Rider IC. (that means Internal Combustion), and would revert to his former trade of Blacksmith Class 2. I remember seeing the memo when Major Stewart showed it to me and said, "D'you know anything about this?"

"What part, sir?"

"The motor cycle bit."

"Oh, yes. I couldn't get it to stop so I ran it into the back of the Colonel's car."

He rubbed his chin. "Yes, I remember. It was the talk of the place. What about this second part. You don't look the blacksmith type to me."

"No, sir."

"Do you know *anything* about blacksmithing?"

"Nothing, sir."

He sighed. "Well, we'll do what we can with you."

"Right, sir."

Now here I was being moved to another REME outfit, hoping that the Records Office in Leicester would get the classification right this time, although I had no idea what it might be. I was sure of one thing — it would not be

Senior Electronics Class 1 Artificer. I would be lucky if I escaped General Duties or the Cookhouse.

The army put me into digs in the little mining village of Forest Hall in the Newcastle area. The army camp was up at Killingworth and I could hardly believe it recently when I visited the place. Forest Hall is no longer there, and even the village of Killingworth itself has been replaced by a New Town spreading out for miles — as though the old Killingworth had been bombed out of existence. After all, Killingworth *was*, among other things, a big ammunition depot. I remember a few of my braver mates during an air raid climbing on to the roofs of the concrete ammo sheds and scooping up and throwing down the small incendiary bombs with shovels!

Forest Hall — may it rest in peace wherever it is now — was a neat little place with rows of miners' houses and the Club at the corner, the chip shop on the other corner and the Co-op midway along the main street, all of them red brick. I was a sergeant at this time and I was told that there was no accommodation available at the camp. So a young, bespectacled lieutenant, Ronnie Hall, took me down to the village with an official list of "available accommodation" houses in his hand. We struck it lucky on the first door-knock.

The woman who opened the door was about six feet tall *and* broad. I heard later that she played left-back for Forest Hall's Women's Football Team; she was also an all-in wrestler. Her name was McGlinchey and she glowered at me before nodding, "All right — bring'm in", and I humped my kitbag and rifle into the little hallway.

I remember the name of the army form but not the number, as Lt. Hall owlishly unfolded it in front of the left-back in her small front parlour. It was headed "Boarding Allowance at the Higher Rate with Meal Service Element". She shot her small eyes down to the bottom right-hand corner of the paper and scrawled her signature hurriedly. I was in.

"Up 'ere," she said when the Lieutenant had gone, and she led the way up the narrow little stairway to a narrow little room facing the rear of the house. "Will you be in for meals durin' the day, d'ye think?"

"No, I don't think so. I'll get lunch at the canteen in the camp."

Little did I know that *that* little arrangement plus the fish and chip shop at the corner probably saved me from malnutrition. This was evident that very evening at six when her husband Peter arrived home from his shift at the mine.

He was a small, bald man with cheeky, bright eyes that were faintly rimmed with coal-dust. He held out his coal-black hand as soon as we met in the little living-room at the rear. "Wye — aye — a sodger, eh? An' a sergeant. Where ye from, son? Glasgow? Man, that's a place an' a half! Glasgow." He pranced about as if dribbling an imaginary football before shooting it into an imaginary net towards the kitchen. "The Rangers! Is that yer team, then? Or Celtic? Eh? Man, that's the place Glasgow! Keep thee feet still Geordie Hinnie!"

It was when we sat down for that first evening meal I knew who was the boss and why Mrs McGlinchey was probably better playing football than in the kitchen. The first course was meat and potatoes with, on the side, a villainous-looking white dumpling which emitted clouds of steam when I cut it open. The inside had a sort of brown, spongy tinge. It tasted dreadful but since the meat was tough and leathery and the potatoes lumpy, it hardly mattered about the dumpling. I hardly ate a mouthful.

Peter saw my reluctance, and while his wife was in the small kitchen he looked at me, screwed up his face and said quietly, "Terrible, isn't it! I've bin havin' that kind of bait for near twenty years. She's a *terrible* cook — *terrible*."

The thirteen-stone left-back heard him and without a word came up from the kitchen and swiped Peter a resounding slap across his ear. While I cowered, waiting for the next blow to hit me simply because I had been a listener, Peter shrugged his slap off and got on with his meal.

Around this time we put together a small band at the camp. I suppose I was the main instigator because I still carried my trumpet around with me in my kitbag, wrapped in a jute sack. Taking this around with me in the bottom of my kitbag was not the most sensible thing in the world because the bell of the instrument had been bashed in twice and beaten out twice by a brass-worker in our workshop. I blessed the day when I was drafted into REME, the army's engineering and workshop division. I was never far away from mobile lathes and hammers and all sorts of tools, to say nothing of the willing craftsmen who just *loved* straightening out a bashed trumpet that had fallen off a truck.

This little band of ours was in demand all over the place. We played at air force bases, naval depots, army camps — all in the evenings when none of us were on duty, all voluntarily and with no privileges of any kind — parade at reveille as usual even if we had been playing at some place miles away till 2 a.m.!

The gig I remember best was the night we played at Blyth Submarine Base. When we reached the big hut which was set up for the dance, the place was crowded with soldiers, naval ratings and air force people of both sexes. Most of the soldiers and the ATS girls were stationed at the base itself and manned the AA guns just outside this hut. Of course everyone knew that this submarine base had been the target for German air raids for weeks but we hoped they would leave our dance alone this particular night.

Of course, the Germans did nothing of the kind and we had the mother and father of a raid halfway through the dance. It was a hair-raiser. Of course when the local alarm sounded, all the personnel — men and women — who made up the gun crews disappeared, and within minutes the 3.7 and 4.5 AA guns were booming to such an extent that I doubt if anyone could hear the band. Certainly my trumpet playing had a distinct tremolo effect and at least twice I dived under the piano while the dancers who were left scuttled for any kind of cover. Fortunately we were not hit and there were no casualties.

Nobody told us that in the next field to the hut there was a Z Battery. This was a unit of about a hundred rockets fired simultaneously during air raids. I remember all of them going off right in the middle of a waltz "I'll Be Loving You Always". We nearly hit the roof with shock.

It was around 1 a.m. when we got our gear together and went out to the truck that would take us home. The driver was a Sergeant Eddie Tucker and he said, "There's a couple of ATS girls want a lift. They're medics working at Longbenton Hospital. I said we'd drop them off".

It was dark inside the truck and I couldn't see the girls. All I saw was the glow of a cigarette one of them was smoking. There were four of us in the band and these two girls, and as the truck sped towards Newcastle in the early hours of the morning, one of the girls was saying, "Well, that was a dance and a half! You could hardly hear the blessed band for the noise of the guns".

"Maybe that was a good thing," said Charlie Park, I suppose trying to fish for a few compliments.

"It certainly *was*," she replied. "Give me Geraldo any time! I never heard such terrible music."

I said nothing and was prepared to keep quiet for the rest of the journey until Miss Grumble started up again. "And that floor! You'd think they might have put some slippy stuff on the floor. In fact, whoever organised that dance should be shot. The sandwiches were terrible and you couldn't tell *what* you were drinking when they poured that stuff called tea."

I had had enough. I said, "Listen, Miss Pernickety. I don't know if anybody's ever told you, but there's a war going on just now. And *you're* damn lucky to be having *any* kind of entertainment. And if *I* had anything to do with organising that dance I'd have made sure *you* weren't invited. *And* you're also damn lucky to be getting

150

a lift home to Longbenton or wherever your unit is."

While her pal remained silent, Miss Grumble exploded, "I don't know who you think you are, Brigadier-General."

Charlie Park said, "If you didn't like our band you should keep your opinion to yourself."

"Ooh, hark at 'im!" she said. "Somebody should give you a penny whistle."

"What's your name?" I asked.

"Semple," she said. "0984530 Nurse Semple. What's yours?"

I told her.

Nobody said anything more for the rest of the journey and we dropped these two nurses at the hospital.

It only took one day for me to get all my rebukes back in my face. The following afternoon I reported to our own small medical unit with stomach pains. It was something I had eaten at lunch in our canteen and the MO insisted I go into — guess where — Longbenton Military Hospital for a few days.

Of course, she knew at once who I was. All she had to do was look at my name and my unit on the sheet at the end of my bed. I didn't have a similar advantage. The nurse's face I saw from the pillow was a pretty one, and not for worlds would I have associated it with the Miss Grumble who sat in the darkness of the truck the previous night. She chose her moment well to tell me her name — when I had the thermometer stuck in my mouth and couldn't say a word.

I am not suggesting that she concocted the foulest-tasting medicine in the hospital specially for my stomach pains but I'll say this — I never in my life swallowed so much of it . . . I'm sure I had four times the average dose. However, one way or another I was cured in a couple of days and back to my unit.

About this time I was getting a bit fed up being stationed constantly in this country. Although I have never been made of hero's stuff nor am I the least bit warlike, I did know that *real* battles were going on abroad — and I just wanted to play at least a small part in them. I applied for a transfer to some unit that might be going "over there" soon. Frankly, I didn't care where I might be posted.

Draft postings were coming through every day to this unit at Killingworth, and although others had their names on the board, mine seemed to take a long time getting there.

One morning about 6 o'clock I was wakened by a Staff Sergeant called Jarvis. He was around my age, perhaps a year or so older, and as he sat on the edge of my bed he certainly looked scared. His face was white and I swear he was shaking slightly.

"I've been posted," he said.

I rubbed my eyes. "Good. Where?"

"The Middle East — somewhere."

"When are you moving?"

I don't think he heard me. "I've been phoning my wife. She's in a terrible state. Y'see we've got two kids."

I sat up, stared at him. "So?"

"Well, you're single." He gulped. "And you're about my age and we're the same classification. I was wondering if I went to see the Sergeant-Major . . ."

"Let me get this straight," I said. "You want me to go in your place?"

"Yes. Y'see, I . . ."

"Okay."

"I've only been married three years . . ." He hadn't heard me.

I swung back my blanket. "Okay. Tell the S.M. I'll go."

He stared at me. "You WILL?"

I reached for my trousers. "Yes. If you're crapping it, I'll go."

There were almost tears in his eyes. "Oh, listen, I knew . . ." "Forget it." I felt a mixture of sickness and sorrow for him.

As it turned out, the Sergeant Major would have none of it. He seemed to recognise at once what Jarvis was up to and he insisted that he go on the draft. I never heard another thing about it, nor did I even speak to anyone about it. I still feel sorry for him. I hope he made it.

In a way this incident brought me to the point of insisting again on a posting to a unit that was going "over there". I was beginning to think that I was to be a permanent soldier-resident in Britain. Although I didn't feel the least bit brave about anything — in fact the air raids themselves on Tyneside scared the daylights out of me — I certainly did NOT want to face the end of the war having had no foreign service at all.

So I insisted. And this time someone must have heard me because I got a posting to a unit mustering down south near Brentwood called the 11th AA Brigade Workshop REME. The Adjutant at Killingworth assured me that this outfit was embarking "very soon". Where? Well, I should know better than *that* to ask such a question. But, yes, they *were* going abroad and, yes, I would get a taste of some frontline stuff.

The 11th Brigade Workshop unit was like a holiday camp. There was only a small staff under a "country gentleman" type of Brigadier and three other officers, and when I arrived I found this small group working in a large commandeered country house. As a Sergeant I was assigned to the REME officer Major Wright.

CHAPTER
SIXTEEN

Doodlebug Days

It would be very comfortable for me now to say that the passage of time has so dimmed my memory of those wartime days that I cannot clearly remember what particular contribution we made to the war effort in that little Brigade HQ. It would also be untrue. Looking back on it now, I really believe that we did very little. It is likely, of course, that my relatively lowly position as a sergeant banished me from the dramatic and momentous decisions taken by our Brigadier and my Major and the other Major, but the truth of the matter is simply that I was hideously underworked. Major Wright came and went mysteriously in a Jeep, sometimes called on me to make a few telephone calls to Woolwich Arsenal, but mostly was away somewhere for days.

The people with whom I shared a workroom were a Warrant Officer called Pike, who was a regular army soldier hailing from Aldershot, a Sergeant Clerk who, looking back on it now, I am sure was gay, and a Corporal who I heard later after we were demobbed became a really big shot with Ford Motor Company.

Nobody bothered whether I was underworked or bored or anything — least of all the Warrant Officer. It was like a sort of secret society. Nobody discussed anything about the war, what we were doing there, where the officers disappeared to, and certainly not what my boss Major Wright did, or what I was expected to do.

We spent a lot of our time moving from one large country house to another. All these moves were to picturesque, beautiful places. The houses, of course, had obviously been commandeered: they were stripped of all furniture, but it meant nevertheless that our living arrangements were usually very good. I have memories of wood pigeons cooing and sunlit evenings and long shadows over magnificent deer parks. I could hardly believe I was on active service at all.

One of the pleasantest places we were stationed at was a little village in Dorset called Tarrant Gunville. We took over the Big House on the outskirts of the village and, like the others, this mansion was superb.

There was a little pub in the village called The Bugle and some of us used to go down of an evening and play darts and shove-halfpenny with the few locals there. Only two years ago, our son and his wife came over to Britain from Canada and we stayed with them in a little village in Hampshire. Looking at the map, I could see that we were not very far from Tarrant Gunville, so we all of us went over there. The village was as quiet and as beautiful as I remembered it from those war days long ago. And The Bugle was still there. But somehow it wasn't the same. Certainly the present owners had preserved much of its character outside, and the interior, typical of pubs in the South of England, was all horse brasses and old prints and oak tables and brick fireplaces. But gone were the soldiers gathered round the fire with leathery, wrinkle-faced locals dipping red-hot pokers into our tankards to bring out the tangy taste of the brew.

The big house on the outskirts of the village was still there but the gates were closed so I had to content myself with a few photographs taken at the entrance to the drive. Since the house was occupied and looked very grand, it is likely that I would not have recognised one inch of the place if we *had* been allowed to enter.

After Tarrant Gunville, the next move ordered by our tweedy Brigadier and his merry majors was to a place in Essex called Hatfield Peverel. This, too, was a pleasant village, and once again we occupied a big estate house. Where on earth the Brigadier got hold of these properties is still a mystery to me. I offered the opinion to Warrant Officer Pike that he consulted the pages of *Country Life*, then asked the War Office to sign a commandeering order. Somehow everywhere we went there were deer parks and beautiful trees and long meadows and sunlit afternoons and lawns.

Of course I got tired of all this milk-and-honey existence so I had a talk with Major Wright.

"What's the matter with you?" he asked. "Don't you like the life with the Brigade?"

"What Brigade?" I asked. "I've never *seen* any army unit except the few of us here. All we seem to do is move from one big house to another all over the South of England. I'm beginning to *feel* like a civvy."

"What's wrong with that? Nice pubs to go to in the evening. Good food. Decent sleeping quarters."

157

"I'm fed up. I want to *do* something for the war thing."

"You don't look the warrior type."

"I'm not," I said. "Not by a long shot. But I just want to do *something* besides drinking pints in village pubs. If it goes on much longer I'll be wearing tweeds or jodhpurs or a hunting outfit."

He sighed. "All right — I'll see what I can do. I have some connections with 21 Army HQ in London."

He had and he did. Within a couple of days I was off to an army barracks at Mill Hill in London where, I was assured, the 22nd Advanced Base Workshop was packing up and "ready to go overseas" any day now. Ready? They were ready for nothing by the looks of things. It was a big outfit with mobile machine tools and all sorts of repair machinery mounted on heavy transporters.

"What're we supposed to be?" I asked Harry Grant, a Sergeant who shared my bunkroom with another two.

"Big mobile workshop," he said. "Repairs on the field. Everything. L.A.D., recovery, complete overhaul of tanks and guns after the battles."

"Sounds big stuff," I said, wondering what *I* was supposed to do when we got "over there".

Of course, they bunged me in an office and I spent nearly all my days organising training on the range and anywhere else the Sergeant Major could think of so that, as he put it, we would be "ninety per cent fighting soldiers and ten per cent workshop people" when we got "over there".

Again, I found that this place was another cushy

number. I got plenty of time off in the evenings and at weekends except for the occasional guard duty. By this time I was engaged to Jean back home in Glasgow and she wrote to me to say that she had volunteered to come down to the London area to serve with the Women's Voluntary Services. Both of us were delighted with this and, providing my orders for "over there" didn't arrive sooner than her visit, both of us could have some time in London in the evenings.

These were the days of the Doodlebugs *and* the V2s, those huge rockets launched from France on London. So you can be sure that our meetings in London were punctuated often by these things. I can remember going for a Chinese meal to Jack Sing's restaurant in Soho and having each of our four courses interrupted by Mr Sing hurrying us down to his cellar because the local street whistles were sounding.

I remember, too, one very anxious time when I caught the tube train and went right over to Victoria where Jean's group were stationed. There was a crowd of worried looking women in the hotel lobby and I grabbed a senior officer.

"What's going on?"

She was grim-faced. "Lewisham."

I remembered what I had heard that very morning back at the camp when I was shaving. It was another Sergeant who told me. A doodlebug had landed in the High Street in Lewisham and gone right through the windows of Woolworths before it exploded. Scores of people were killed and injured.

"What about it?" I asked.

"The girls we sent out there yesterday haven't returned."

"Was Jean McLean one of them?"

"Yes, she was."

"Have you found out . . . ?"

"No, we haven't. You'll just have to wait until we get word with the rest of us."

I sat down and waited and waited. Every time someone walked in the hotel door to the lobby I got to my feet and followed them to try and hear if there was any news. Nothing.

Then, at long last, a group of women walked into the hotel and Jean was in the middle of the group. They had stayed in Lewisham to give some help before coming back to Victoria.

Eventually the 22 ABW did indeed get "over there". Although I half-expected that we might go to the Middle East, the destination was to be no further than France — or Holland, or Belgium — at any rate somewhere on Mainland Europe. Our date of departure was a little while after D-Day.

There was a tremendous scurry of activity at Mill Hill — loading vehicles, packing equipment, parading, and getting our huge machine tools — lathes and grinders and presses and borers — on to low-loaders. We rolled away one Tuesday morning and our convoy was about a mile long.

The first place we reached was a large mustering area near Portsmouth where we put up under canvas. It seemed to me that the whole of the British army was there: there were miles of tents and trucks. Perhaps my guess was nearer the truth than I imagined because I learned later that this area was indeed the main trooping place for all the convoys going over to France.

Busty Overton was the driver on my truck and I remember how I felt when we were on the landing craft going across the Channel — goosy and thrilled and apprehensive. When we were within sight of the French coast we could see and hear the firing of artillery. Apparently this was coming from German forces entrenched near Le Havre. Funnily enough, although these shells were uncomfortably close at times to our convoy of landing craft, I didn't feel the least nervous. Indeed, I preferred *this* kind of activity under fire than those wretched V1s and V2s we had been experiencing back in the London area. The artillery shells along this part of the French coast were "open" and somehow "healthier".

None of that German bombardment hit any of our craft as we approached the beach. It was at this stage, before the first whistle was sounded, that I said to Busty, "Go over that bit again."

"Wot bit?"

"The bit about what the man said when we were in Portsmouth about sealing the distributor with that putty stuff."

"Well, I did."

"Did what?"

"Sealed it. With that stuff — so it's watertight".

"You're sure?"

"Certain. When this truck goes off the boat, it'll go right under the water."

"And keep going? Right up the beach."

"Right. I know as well as you do what'll happen if we stick. But it won't."

"And it'll keep going?"

"Sarge," said Busty, a slight tremor in his voice, "You know what we both need?"

"Yes, I do."

He reached into his hip pocket and produced a half-bottle of Johnny Walker, uncorked it and handed it to me. "Get a belt of that."

I did and so did he. Then the first whistle sounded, the front of our craft clanged down, truck engines were revving and Busty put ours in gear. We crawled to the open doors, the truck went down under the water, Busty accelerated and we kept crawling up the sand and pebbles. We kept going all the way to the shelter of the trees. Neither of us said anything until we reached the trees with the other vehicles.

Before we embarked we had been given mass instruction on how to use the K-Pack. This was a tightly compacted box of emergency rations, most of the food dehydrated into what looked like chunks of wood. Only the different colours of the "wood" could tell you whether you were handling steak mince or pork or anything else.

Our convoy was about half a mile long; indeed it really was a complete engineering repair factory on wheels, and mounted on the vehicles were lathes, milling machines, presses, grinders — everything for the major repair of tanks and artillery.

We rolled on towards Caen and Bayeux with no

hindrance, no enemy action and certainly no enemy aircraft because by this time the Luftwaffe had been cleared out of the skies in this part of France.

Then we stopped and a motor cyclist roared down the column to tell us it was time to eat. Bravely I got out my K-Pack, and a few of the others gathered round to see the miracle food being prepared.

I think I did everything I had been shown in Portsmouth. I set up the tiny stove, inserted the fuel disc, lit it, put my billycan on it, half-filled with sterilised water. When I looked up there were eight pairs of eyes above unshaven chins watching me suspiciously. One of the soldiers licked his lips and said hoarsely, "What're you makin', sergeant?"

I stirred the billycan of water with a spoon expertly.

"Mince."

"Mince?"

"With doughballs?" said another.

"I think so." I took out the thing that looked like a block of wood from the box and started paring slivers off it into the billycan. The slivers floated on the surface.

"What's that?" said another hungry soldier.

"It says mince on the pack."

Nothing happened. The chips of "wood" kept floating on the sterilised water and the eight very hungry soldiers were getting restless.

"Did you watch the man doing it back at Portsmouth?"

"What's supposed to happen?"

"How the hell's that going to turn into mince?"

"Where are the doughballs?"

"What's for 'afters', Sarge? Is it that chunk of mahogany?"

"Is it supposed to turn into a pumpkin?"

I remembered that I had a large jar of Bovril in my kitbag so, in desperation, I got it out and emptied the stuff into the billycan. Eventually it all thickened and I tasted it. It was abominable and I sat back while eight angry faces looked at me.

"When are we eating, Sarge?" Just then we heard the motor cycle roaring down the convoy again. This time the rider had a huge bag of sandwiches. He stopped and threw us a bundle of them. "Here," he shouted. "Nobody can get that bloody K-Pack to work. Cook's sent these."

CHAPTER
SEVENTEEN

France

Fortunately some other unit had buried the Canadians before we got there. I am not sure who buried the Germans but I am certain of one thing — there must have been the mother and father of all battles in that place just a few days before our convoy trundled through the village.

It was called Cormelles and I know it is still there just outside Caen because my daughter and her family were on holiday in Normandy two years ago and she actually phoned me from there; she knew I would be interested to hear her speaking from the little place which was virtually my home for a whole winter during the war.

As I remember it, the village was on a main road used by trucks and tanks and guns night and day going up to the fighting still going on near Bayeux. We settled down with our two miles of mobile workshop in an area which looked as if it had once been an industrial estate — that was before the Germans and the Canadians blew half of it up. We set up tents for half the unit and the other half got into buildings of some kind that were weatherproof. I was one of the lucky ones and got a bed rigged up in a wooden hut.

Nothing much happened to us during these days. The

Germans were still being pushed further into France somewhere and the tanks and trucks and guns kept rolling up through the village. The mud was feet deep and we nearly lost one of our sergeants, Busty Nicholl, when he was out looking for booze. He was about sixty — we never knew how he got into the army — and was drunk most of the time on anything that could be swallowed and allowed life to continue. Busty fell in the mud in what was a ditch almost up to his neck. We fished him out with a recovery rig and equipped him with a whistle to hang round his neck in case of future accidents.

One day I was on guard duty at our vehicle park when I saw two Frenchmen wandering among the trucks. I approached them and asked them what they were looking for. The older man had no English but the young one — he looked a bit like Maurice Chevalier — spoke English very well and he had a nice smile. "We just look, Sergeant."

"What're you looking for?"

He shrugged. "We look for the end of the war, n'est ce pas?"

"You can say that again."

We talked on and after ten minutes he had invited me to join his family for lunch the following Sunday. "And you bring a friend with you." He gave me an address on the outskirts of Caen.

The following Sunday I brought Tommy York with me. He was a Sergeant and a good friend. So we got a jeep and drove to the address. As I half expected, this particular street was a ruin. Most of the houses had been shelled. Then I saw the two figures coming towards me. The younger one — more like Maurice Chevalier than ever — was smiling again. He wore a skipped seaman's cap and the older man — he was his father — wore a battered straw hat.

The younger man's name was Pierre and his father Jean. Pierre held out his hand. "Welcome. You come with us."

Their home was a converted railway carriage in the middle of a piece of waste ground surrounded by deserted and bombed buildings. As we approached it, Tommy said to me, "I hope you know what you're getting us into."

"It's a free nosh," I said. "Sunday dinner."

"What're you up to?"

"Nothing. All I want is somebody to do my weekly wash while we're here."

"For what?"

"Forty cigarettes a week. That's the going rate."

"I knew you were up to something."

"I'm not usually as brainy as this. But I'm fed up boiling my clothes in a biscuit tin then hanging them up on the tent ropes every week."

"If they agree, put in a word for me. I'm fed up doing my own as well."

I don't think I've had a meal to equal it since. The whole family were there, gathered round a long table lengthwise along the railway carriage — grandparents, mamma, pappa, the grandchildren, brothers, sisters, aunts and uncles. For a moment I thought it was a wedding feast. It was an epicurean paradise of about ten courses with all kinds of wines followed by coffee and cigars.

When the meal was over, Pierre poured more coffee and invited me through to the next room. I didn't know there was a next room but I had misjudged the length of the railway carriage. We went through to an elongated parlour where he offered me another cigar and poured a glass of cognac. I should have known there was something coming; he had obviously chosen me rather than Tommy because I looked softer and more gullible. He was probably right.

Pierre leaned forward a bit and held up his thumb and forefinger, rubbing them together. "You like to make some money?"

"Money? Well — not — I'm not sure — How?"

"Essence." His lips uttered the word quietly.

"Essence? You mean petrol?"

He nodded.

"Where would I get petrol?"

He shrugged and raised his eyebrows good-humouredly. Then he spread his open hand out upside down and waggled it backwards and forward. I may have been simple but not entirely stupid. I stood up. "Sorry, Pierre, you're not on. I couldn't, I shouldn't and I won't."

He beamed like a cherub and held out his hand. "I understand. No hard feelings, eh?"

"None. It was a great meal." I took his hand. "What about forty cigarettes a week to do my washing?"

"But of course." He put his arm round my shoulder as we left the room. "My wife — she do that. Forty cigarettes."

"And my pal. Another forty fags?"

"But of course." He held the door open. "Come through. I will explain all about us, eh?"

What a story he told. Pierre and his family were carnival people. All their roundabouts and helter-skelters and machinery were buried — yes, *buried* — under a field somewhere in Brittany. Now that the end of the war was in sight, they wanted to dig it all up and get back into business. And they needed petrol — gallons of it. Pierre thought I might be a soft touch.

We remained good friends and Tommy and I got our washing done every week. But we never did get a ten-course meal again.

Before we left France I nearly got a medal. It happened this way. General Patten US had apparently run his army as far as the outskirts of Paris. He also ran out of fuel and ammunition and supplies. So the word came down to our unit — "Get some of these tank low-loaders converted into carriers to transport jerricans of petrol and other supplies up to Patten's army".

I must have temporarily gone out of my mind to get involved in this project. But we had a welding expert called Sergeant Buckley who stood up in the mess one evening and said, "I need volunteers to weld sides on to these tank low-loaders round the clock. Then they get loaded and sent on their way up front to the Americans. Who'll volunteer?"

"Who does the welding?" shouted someone.

"You do. I'll show you how to handle the torch."

"Working at night as well?" asked another.

"Night and day — till the job's done."

"What about the Germans?"

"Their air force is finished. There'll be no air raids."

As I say, I had a brainstorm and held up my hand. The job was simple enough once I got the hang of the welding torch. The welds were crude but held the sides of the loaders together. We worked round the clock and stopped only for snack meals and an occasional snooze. Incidentally, Sergeant Buckley worked so hard himself that he went blind temporarily.

Weeks later some minor decorations and recognitions were awarded. I think Buckley got quite an important medal. I'm not sure who else got what, but I'm quite glad my little contribution passed unnoticed. In that war I never was the medal type for anything and I didn't want to spoil my record.

There was one building in Cormelles more or less intact — the auditorium. Goodness knows what it was used for before the Germans moved into the area but there was no doubt what *they* used it for. They probably had assemblies and meetings and Heil Hitler booster sessions in that hall. Above the stage there was still the huge insignia of the swastika and the eagle's wings. It was in this huge hall that we ran our own assemblies when there was something important to bring the troops together.

For some reason our Colonel — he was a Sandhurst man — got the idea that I was good at communications so he called me into his office one afternoon and said, "What d'you know about V.D., Sergeant?"

"I know *I* haven't got it, sir."

"I should hope not. The Americans in Italy are riddled with it. It's an epidemic there."

"Well, they should be careful . . ."

"Yes, yes. Don't give me any of that moralising twaddle. The point is that we're not having it here."

"Where, sir?"

"Here — in this unit."

I stared at him. I wondered what on earth he wanted *me* to do. I said, "Well, I don't think there's much chance of *that* in this place, sir."

"We're not taking any chances. And I want *you* to do something about it. Get a driver and ferret around the district. There must be *some* unit or medical outfit somewhere with films on the subject. You know the sort of thing — something to scare the hell out of them."

It was Busty Overton who found the place — an American gunnery unit over by Mondeville. I saw a Captain and asked if he had any films on the subject.

"Sure," he said. "Got a projector?"

"No, sir. But we have a hall."

He bawled into an office building and a gangly Corporal appeared. The captain said, "Get this guy a film projector and a couple of these V.D. films. You know the ones." He gave the corporal an old-fashioned look.

I had no time to preview the film. The Colonel wanted the show to be put on that evening. So we rigged up the projector, found a Lance-Corporal who could work the thing, gave him the reels and watched the hundreds of soldiers filing into the hall. Then the lights faded out and the screening started.

I could hardly believe what I was seeing on the screen.

After a time all I was aware of was the sound of soldiers either hurrying out of the hall or being sick where they sat. It was without doubt the most horrific visual description of anything I have ever seen — before or since. I think the title of the thing was "Short Shanker" or something like that. The other one was just as bad and I know that two of our men fainted in their seats.

Whether because of my role as a V.D. impresario or lack of opportunity in the district, I never heard of one case of venereal disease all the time we were there.

It was around this time I founded a weekly newspaper. It may surprise you to know that the last people to know about the progress of a war are the people in it. At least, that was my impression. In spite of the well-meaning and well-trumpeted efforts of the army communication services with their professional material, the men in our unit were mostly in the dark about many things. Not matters of high intelligence or strategy or where Montgomery's forces might strike next — just news about what was happening back home or in the next hut.

I found an old duplicator in the building we used as an office and I already had access to a typewriter. All I needed was paper, and Busty Overton and I found it ten miles away in a disused paper mill which had been taken over by the Americans. They let us take away as much duplicating paper as we wanted.

I called the newspaper *The Craftsman* simply because we were a workshop unit. I typed the columns, drew the pictures, wrote the stories and ran it off. I worked after my daily grind at night and distributed it around the camp. It was an instant success for one simple reason — there was nothing else. Of course, the whole thing was very, very localised and in places almost like a school newspaper. But it was what the soldiers wanted.

CHAPTER
EIGHTEEN

How I Nearly Met General Montgomery

We moved into Belgium in the spring. We took a week to pack up everything — machine tools and recovery vehicles and generators and workshop equipment of every shape and size. The place where we set up for business again was a little village outside Brussels called Ruisbroek. We took over an engineering factory called Société Gregg which had been in turn commandeered by the Germans. The place was ideal for repairing tanks and guns. There was only one snag — there was no accommodation for us. So we pitched our tents again in a field nearby and there we stayed for months.

Of course, I took *The Craftsman* with me. But I had no duplicator or paper supply. Although I was doing this sort of thing after duty in the evenings, I began to wonder if I could expand the thing and have the newspaper produced professionally.

I borrowed a bicycle one Sunday and went round the district looking for possible clues. I found what I was looking for in the town along the canal bank called Halle. There was a printing shop with a house right above it opposite the cathedral. And it was obvious from the items in the shop window that they did a lot of religious work for the church. I hoped that their tastes and abilities were sufficiently catholic to embrace my little British army unit newspaper. So I rang the bell.

The middle-aged lady who opened the door spoke no English, nor could she get along with my schoolboy French. So she called her daughter who spoke all three languages. The name was Demesmaeker and the family consisted of Mamma, who was a widow, two sons and a daughter. I was invited into the house and, Sunday or no Sunday, I found myself dealing with them. One six-page newspaper once a week printed in English (as translated for the compositor by the daughter) for eighty cigarettes and a tin of coffee. Done. Start next Friday.

It was a great adventure. Now that I had professional printing, I could run all sorts of columns — advice to the lovelorn, news from back home, sports news, even sales and wants ads for various things. I got the cigarettes and the coffee from the unit stores on a special chit from the Colonel and I had my own transport — a bicycle with a rear carrier box. I cycled backwards and forwards along that canal bank twice a week, and between them the Demesmaekers composed the type in English.

There are copies of this newspaper today in the files of the British Museum, and many months later in Germany, when the General Election was under way in Britain, I wrote a letter each to Sir Winston Churchill and Clement Attlee asking for a message for the troops in our unit. Each sent me a brief letter promising a land of hope and glory if the soldiers would vote for their party. I published both letters side by side in the next issue.

After the war, the BBC asked me to write a documentary of the life of this little newspaper. I did this (on our honeymoon) and it was broadcast.

But back in Belgium when I had the paper produced on a proper printing press and expanded it to six pages, I got a volunteer staff around me to help with the production. Tommy Rork was Chief Sub, or something or other, while two pals did various jobs.

The war was coming to an end by this time — as was our little newspaper. When our unit packed up again and set off for Germany across the Rhine, I realised we had one more issue to run. An official dictum came from on high: "No unauthorised publications are to be published in Germany." And that was that.

The place where we settled down was called Finkenvarder. It was a small town — about the size of Govan, in Glasgow — down the Elbe, and it was quite plain what they did here. The Blom and Voss shipbuilding yards dominated everything; and this is where we installed our machinery and equipment, to repair tanks supposedly for use in the still-raging Japanese war. (We learned later that the tanks we restored — with our unit name on them — were left rusting in a field near Hanover.)

Finkenvarder was a typical industrial riverside town. It reminded me of Jarrow on Tyneside: dull and dreary. The people we saw occasionally about the cobbled street looked sullen and cheerless. (Who wouldn't be after the horrendous firebomb raids on Hamburg and all along the river?) They were also starving, and we doled out such food as we could spare, specially to the children.

Our billets were de luxe. We simply took over the German Marine Barracks nearby. We were told that this was where the submarine crews ate and slept when they were ashore. After two successive winters under canvas the place was a palace to us — polished floors, clean, wide corridors, mess rooms and dining areas like those in a hostel. We wallowed in the comfort.

I remember taking a ferryboat trip down the Elbe one Saturday afternoon towards Hamburg, and I could hardly believe what I was seeing. The devastation was tremendous — huge cranes dangling in tangled messes over the river, pylons down, great bomb craters in the yards and wreckage everywhere on either side. The ferry reached the Bismarck statue in the city and I disembarked with the Germans as casually as if I were coming off the Whiteinch ferry on the Clyde back home. Nobody spoke to me. I was offered no hostility or greeting. Nothing. I remember a saying of my mother's, "Whit's fur ye'll no' go bye ye". It meant that whatever's in store for you won't go past you. This seemed to be true during those few months in Finkenvarder. And it happened this way.

I nearly became involved in an international incident. And in a way I am sorry I didn't, because it would have been the one and only event of any importance in the whole of my undistinguished army career during that war. The Blom and Voss works were world-famous; for Germans they were the nation's pride and joy. By the time we had taken them over, they had been in the process of building the largest seaplanes in the world. Indeed we saw the prototypes in their hangars and I have never seen any plane before or since so huge. The wingspan was incredible. They had been working on this for two years before we got there.

Now there wasn't much doubt whose spoils of war was Blom and Voss. The works were well and truly in the British sector, just a few miles downriver from Hamburg. Normally there would have been no problem about who should take them over and administer the situation. But these were not normal times. There were faint signs of the beginning of the Cold War. And the Russians said they wanted Blom and Voss. We said "no way", or something like that. So a big meeting was called somewhere in Germany between senior Russian officers and British generals, including General Montgomery.

I knew nothing about all these shenanigans until the Colonel called me into his office one afternoon, explained what was going on, and asked me if I could prepare a brochure containing a complete write-up about the place, how our unit took it over and generally giving an argument in favour of the British. And it was to be illustrated with photographs.

I was amazed. But I said I'd do my best. I had visions of being decorated with a Victoria Cross by Monty himself at a special ceremony in Whitehall in London.

The first thing I did was to get myself into Hamburg. I sought out a photographic agency, spoke in English to the head photographer, got his agreement and yanked him off to a special branch of Intelligence whose offices were in Hamburg. I had been given this address and I waited while he was questioned and vetted for over an hour. Then he was given a special pass and handed back to me.

His name was Hans, and we got along very well together. He could speak good English and we set to work going round all the massive complex of Blom and Voss. He took the pictures and I did the write-up. Then we put the whole thing together — six copies — and I delivered them to the Colonel and paid off the photographer.

I thought that was the end of my part in the affair until Hogmanay, the evening before New Year's Day, which, as every sensible person knows, is sacred to most Scots. There was I in the Sergeants' Mess knocking back pint after pint of excellent German beer when the colonel walked in. (It is the custom in the British Army for the Sergeants' Mess to have "open house" to officers on Hogmanay.) I thought he had just dropped in for a tipple when he came right over to me. "Good, you're here, Sergeant. Get your small kit and get yourself off to this address near Detmold." He handed me a slip of paper and a letter of authorisation for the army railway people in Hamburg.

"When, sir?"

"Now."

"Now? On Hogmanay?"

"Right. Sorry, but it can't be helped. You're to take four copies of that brochure to General Montgomery's headquarters in Bad Oynasan so that he gets them in the morning. He'll be with British officials at a meeting tomorrow negotiating with the Russians, I think. Anyway, he needs these brochures first thing tomorrow."

I collected the brochures from the Colonel's office.

They were in a leather satchel. I got my own small side-kit together and I set off down to the ferryboat on our side of the river. I had to waken the skipper, who was in a drunken sleep in the cabin, and he started up the engine to get me across to the other side. Then I got a very late suburban train into Hamburg and reported to the R.T.O. at Altona station. An officer there knew all about my mission (the Colonel had probably telephoned him) and he said, "The only train I can get you on is a D.P. one."

"What's that?"

"Displaced persons. It'll be packed with them — they come from all over Europe. So don't be surprised."

He was right. Every carriage seemed full of men and women and children, but I managed to squeeze my way into a seat at the end of a row of them. Heaven knows where they came from. They could have been Hungarians or Czechs or Russians or simply Jews from the camps.

There was a military car waiting for me at Detmold station in the grey of dawn. The driver said little as he drove up into the spa country. Then we reached the General's eyrie — a small castle with turrets and well-kept grounds and a pebbled driveway. Very nice.

The Major I saluted at a desk in a back room held out his hand for the satchel. "You've got the four copies, Sergeant?"

"Yes, sir." I handed it over. Then, as he opened it, I took a long shot: "I'm supposed to hand them over to General Montgomery."

The major wasn't born yesterday. "No, you were not.

You'll leave them with me." Then he smiled broadly. "It was a good try. When're you getting out?"

"On demob? In two weeks."

"Got small kit with you? Good. I'll telephone your CO and say you're having a holiday here for a week. The sergeant-major'll show you where you kip and eat. Okay?"

I smiled. "Suits me, sir."

And that was that. I never did get to see General Montgomery but I did have a great time in that place for a week. The beer was free and each meal was like a banquet. There were about thirty army people of all ranks in that castle living in high style, and I joined them for my "holiday". We did no work — just ate and drank and slept and played football and darts and read. Then I got a train back to my unit in Finkenvarder.

I was out in less than a week. I came home by train after train . . . queuing in station after station . . . eating in a dozen different canteens . . . until I got to the big demob centre in England where thousands of us got our civilian demob clothing.

My father and mother by this time had moved back to a room-and-kitchen in Maryhill. My father always said, anyway, that he never wanted to be away from the sound of the Glasgow tramcars. I found them on the main road just a few yards round the corner from Braeside Street.

Of course they were glad to see me. And they said nothing when I changed into my civilian demob suit etc. But my mother got my army greatcoat dyed navy blue. And it was this outfit plus my felt hat which nearly confined me to a life of bachelorhood. The first time Jean saw me she said she nearly ran a mile. I looked like a bookie's runner. There was only one saving grace about those days — nearly everyone around my age was wearing a demob suit, although I never did see another dyed army greatcoat. And the hat was no better or worse than the thousands of felt monstrosities out on the streets every day. But the outfit did nothing for the resumption of my love life. By the time we were married a few months later everything was dumped — suit, coat, hat, even the shoes. It took me longer to get used to a soft bed.

CHAPTER
NINETEEN

Home? Where's Home?

For a single serviceman during that war leave was a solid bore after a couple of days. All right, we said hello to our parents and they hugged us and we felt great as returning warriors even although we might have spent the last six months peeling potatoes or pushing a pen.

Certainly I had the added spice of finding out where my home was nearly every time I came home on leave. That first leave from Orkney had me tracking all over Glasgow after I found our room-and-kitchen house shattered by bombing before I tracked my parents down in Coatbridge. My next leave was spent in a spare room of a nice couple, again in Coatbridge where my parents had gone. The one after that was to a two-room house in Maryhill Road just round the corner from Braeside Street. And — glory be — this is where I found them on subsequent homecomings.

Two memorable things happened to me on leave during those war years. My wife warns me that they are *never* to be linked or even seen in the same context even although both took place within the one fortnight.

One of the main reasons why home leave for a single soldier was always a pain was the simple fact that only a miracle caused any of his pals' leave from the services to coincide with his own. But this is what happened to me on this particular period — two of my best friends, Alex and Willie Corrigan, were home at the same time as me. So we met every other evening in Wypers Pub in Renfield Street and went to a cinema or a dance or played billiards.

One particular night, there we were standing at the bar with pints of beer when Willie said, "What'll we do tonight?"

Alex said, "Why don't we go to a music hall?"

"A what?"

"Variety. At the Pavilion Theatre up the road. We haven't been to a theatre show in years."

"Great," said I.

The billboards outside the theatre showed the usual listing of sketches and turns — dancers and comics and jugglers. And heading the bill was a famous tenor singer, Peter Gourley, who had a wide reputation for his romantic and soul-touching songs. A favourite saying then among theatre goers was that when Peter Gourley started to sing, "there wasn't a dry eye in the house".

I learned later that on the Monday, Tuesday and Wednesday of that week he had had rapturous applause for his rendering of a cowboy western song "The Last Roundup". This was a sad song about a cowboy leading his horse on the last round-up of his career. And the significant line was "Gert along, li'l dogie, gert along..." This was the Thursday evening and it had been decided by the management that the song would be more effective if he appeared on the stage holding the reins of a horse.

In those war-restricted days, of course, it was almost impossible to find any stage-trained animals, specially at short notice. So the manager had a brainwave and he arranged for one of the big Clydesdale horses from the LNER goods depot in Buchanan Street to be hired out for the occasion.

This was the night I was there with my two pals. When it came to Peter Gourley's turn, there was tremendous applause to welcome a singer everyone loved. The curtains opened and there stood Peter dressed in a cowboy outfit nonchalantly holding the reins of this huge Clydesdale with the golden sunset of an Arizona prairie and cactus plants as a background. The audience listened with heartfelt reverence as he began to sing. Then my eyes gazed at the stage in disbelief. The horse began to piss all over the stage.

I learned two things from this shocking incident. First, we couldn't hear the singer over the deafening noise of the horse doing what comes naturally. Second — and this really amazed me — we couldn't see the singer. Great clouds of steam enveloped him. But worse was to come. Peter Gourley managed to signal to the stage hands through the clouds. They hastily dropped the curtain on the Arizona sunset to cut out the still-peeing horse. This left the singer gallantly mouthing his song. Then an enormous puddle of water appeared, spreading from under the curtain. This reached the footlights and instantly we were all left in blackness as every light in the house fused.

The three of us never stopped laughing for days. I haven't quite got over it even now. And the incident really made my whole leave worthwhile. Well, almost.

What made it really worthwhile for the rest of my life was a dance we attended in the Glasgow School of Art the following evening. It was here I met my wife. But — I repeat — over all those years she has absolutely forbidden me to tell one story with the other. I hope I have sufficiently divided the two evenings to satisfy her.

But leaves were leaves and no soldier in his right mind would refuse one. What dismayed me time after time were the topics of importance to my parents. It always amazed me how I could return from anywhere — and it might have been Burma for all the interest it created — and listen for an hour to my mother telling me about their latest row with Aunt Kate, or my father telling me how the proletariat would form a dictatorship after the war, starting, no doubt, in Maryhill. Everything was so parochial, so small, yet so important to *them*. I suppose I might have had the same petty interests had I remained at home rather than joining the army.

I'm not surprised today when I hear and see evidence of mocking the participants in the last war. Most of it — television skits and the like — is harmless enough and typically British in making fun of bad national experiences. To my mind, all this is fair in love and war.

There is, however, a less agreeable attitude expressed by people who knew nothing of the war, either because they were too young or, more likely now, because they were not around. And there are fewer and fewer of us left to offer any other opinion or to remind anyone what was at stake.

However well expressed were the opinions of our leaders then, and the propaganda which was distributed, ordinary soldiers said very little about why we were in the thing at all. Of course, there was conscription and we would have been in harness one way or another to help with the war effort. But among my mates back in our unit, or at home with my pals, or with my relatives, I rarely heard anyone question the purpose of the conflict. Even those — like my mother — who knew little about the purpose of the German Nazi machine, never questioned for a minute who was the enemy and why we were at war.

There were many reasons for this, apart from the natural reticence of ordinary people over deep feelings of patriotism or right and wrong. We were all too busy getting on with our work and staying alive and getting food and getting sleep at night. War was more a condition of living than any grand catastrophe. Indeed, there was a time in France when I began to imagine that *this* was normality and that periods of peace were things to be looked forward to: "I wonder when the next peace will be."

When I was in Belgium I managed to get a copy of a lengthy German document translated into English, which set out the intentions of the Germans after Britain was conquered. It made my hair curl. All males of a certain age-band thus and so . . . all females of certain ages thus and so . . . Without doubt every man, woman and child in Britain was to be subservient to the Greater German Reich — virtually slaves. Nobody likes to talk about these things now — least of all the

Germans themselves, none of whom in this generation had anything to do with such an atrocious government as the Nazi one. But when I hear or see the courage and the determination of millions of ordinary people during those terrible years being lampooned or ridiculed beyond the bounds of good comedy, I can get very angry even although my contribution to the war effort was about the most meagre imaginable.

It is possible that old soldiers have been saying this sort of thing after their wars since time began.

It was the British Navy which introduced me to strong drink. I was twenty-two when I was stationed in Orkney. Our little unit went up there in January 1940 in the middle of a winter so cold that part of the sea was frozen around Stromness. As I related before, the snow was piled feet high, the marines took our kitbags to the Faroes in error and we were sleeping rough in an old disused distillery. As we said then to ourselves, it was an LBU developing into an MBU — a large balls-up developing into a monumental balls-up. And once again everybody was in the same boat. Everyone was so cold that nobody talked about it.

For some reason, the army were under the command of the Senior Service in Orkney — something to do with the sanctity of Scapa Flow and the fleet anchored within those sixty-eight islands. That was why the soldiers wore an "anchor" arm-badge, and why we saluted naval officers when we met them.

The only advantage any of us could see in being under naval command happened one night when the temperature was below any tolerable level. Many soldiers couldn't sleep because of the cold, and one of my pals nearly died — of pneumonia. Then came the news — the navy were issuing a rum ration. Within minutes the word spread all over Stromness and queues were forming in the snow as tots of rum as thick as varnish were doled out. Two of my mates were strictly teetotal and gave me their tots to add to my own. I slept like a log that night.

That introduction to alcohol didn't drive me to drink. Indeed I didn't taste drink again for months until I got to the unit in Newcastle where I was introduced to a deadly mess game — Cardinal Puff. There was a ritual of signs and recitations; and if you were in the hot seat and forgot one of these things or made the slightest mistake, your beer glass was topped up and you had to begin again. It's a good cure for over-indulgence.

The next significant binge I remember was in France shortly after we had settled into our hut in Cormelles. One of our Sergeants put the hat round for coffee or cigarettes or chocolates, then went out with his bounty into the village to try and find somebody who would trade some booze for his goodies. As soon as he had gone, an orderly appeared at our hut door and said, "Who's Duty Sergeant?"

"I am," said Jimmy Cooksley.

"Well, there's a ten-tonner broken down at our gates on the main road. It's a broken axle and he's asking if we can fix it."

"We don't open for business till next week," said Cooksley. "Tell the driver to find the nearest LAD. We're not geared for quick fixes."

The orderly grinned. "It's a beer truck, sergeant."

There was a silence while this statement sank in. "And he's got barrels and barrels of it. He's taking it up to the lines past Bayeux! An' he says if he doesn't deliver it by morning they'll hang him. It's for the HLI."

Three sergeants almost jammed themselves in the doorway as they hurried out. I was one of them. The truck was tilted right over in a deep ditch and the driver was standing beside it, knee-deep in mud.

Cooksley said, "How many barrels 'ave you got?"

"Ten, sergeant."

Cooksley held up two fingers without saying a word. The driver smiled and shrugged. "What's the difference to the HLI? Beer's beer. You're on."

The deed was done. We got the truck on its way within hours and we got two large barrels — one for us and one for the orderly who would dispense its contents to his mates.

Our barrel was marked all round its edge "Bass XXX Specially Brewed For The Industrial Area of Britain" or words like that.

When we got it back to our hut, Sergeant Cavendish had returned from his trading expedition with a small firkin of Calvados which is really a Normandy distilled applejack in its crudest form. So we decided to have a party. Our beer should have been left for twenty-four hours to settle. We left it about ten minutes while we fixed a tap on the barrel. The ration to each sergeant was one pint of unsettled Bass with one glass of Calvados. So we had our party and I often feel that if the Germans in the Ardennes had decided to break through that night, there was one link in the chain of defence that would have melted in a haze of alcohol.

When I woke in the morning I looked around our hut and saw a dozen death-heads. I thought that *I* had died and this was me in Hades.

It cured me for life of many things to do with drinking.

CHAPTER
TWENTY

First Report from Hell

For many years after the war I kept telling friends at home that the main reason I started that little newspaper, *The Craftsman*, was because the men in our unit and those in nearby outfits were getting no real information about the progress of the war. I kept telling myself this too, until I woke up one day and realised that *that* was only part of the truth. The other part was that none of us in that unit or around us seemed to *want* to know anything about the war. We were just not very interested. Life was a daily grind, and keeping warm in winter and getting enough to eat and keeping out of trouble seemed to be our only interests.

So that I could get my bearings right while strolling down memory lane recently, I went through a few issues of that little newspaper to see what I *did* publish — mainly "lists" extracted from BBC radio reports and from the British daily papers.

The Germans surrendered at Stalingrad. That "other" war on the Russian front filled us with horror at times. It was quite clear that the war's end was at least in sight, although the Germans were now conscripting everyone who could carry a gun, even boys and old men. There was a new term being used in the papers — "unconditional surrender" — and it was obvious that there would be no repeat of the last war's Versailles armistice fiasco.

In North Africa, Tripoli fell to the allies and Tunisia was taken under General Alexander. Most of the Germans in Italy surrendered and every news bulletin on the radio brought better and better news — at least so far as *our* part of the world was concerned. It was another matter in the Far East. Mountbatten was appointed Chief of all South East Asia Command. The Japs were still dangerously near Australia but we were trying to get them out of New Guinea. As allies, the Chinese were helping us in Burma.

Il Duce, Mussolini, fled with his mistress and was assisted in his escape by the Germans. The German air force was virtually no more — and this is why in our workshop unit we could quite calmly work at night using flares and welding equipment.

All this was the Big Scene which I tried to encapsulate and bring into focus in my little duplicated newspaper. But a quick readership survey round the huts and in the mess in the evening soon told me that what they wanted to read were the juicy little pieces from their own home towns. Since this would have required me to cover about a hundred locations in the UK and extend the pages of the newspaper to about two hundred, they had to swallow what I gave them of international news, or lump it. Generally speaking, they accepted exactly what I printed.

One thing was dominant in everybody's mind that year in France — when would we be demobbed? Even home leave didn't have the same attractions although few of us had the opportunity. What everyone wanted was OUT!

That was until the Ardennes breakout became a fact. We could hardly believe the news that the German forces deep in the Ardennes in Belgium had launched a punching attack which, at one stage, looked as though it might get to the coast and cut much of the allied forces off. It was as ominous as that.

We had attached to our camp about a thousand German prisoners of war and our unit was charged with *keeping* them prisoners. They lived in huts on the perimeter and we guarded them constantly on a rota basis.

One day there was a tremendous hullabaloo and many of us were ordered out on special guard duty, fully armed. Timed almost to the minute, many of these prisoners had produced radio transmitters which they had built themselves; they also had home-made weapons like swords and daggers. Naturally we organised a hut-by-hut search and confiscated about a ton of material. After that they quietened down and, as we learned later, the Ardennes offensive was beaten back.

All this was followed by a second attempt on Hitler's life in Germany. Like the first, it failed, and the perpetrators were cruelly executed. Things were getting desperate for the Nazis. Leningrad was relieved after months of siege. Our troops entered Rome. Paris was delivered from German hands and suicide squads of Germans were formed to try to stem the tide of the allied advance through France. General de Gaulle was in New York and got a rapturous reception.

Back home, however, the war was anything but over. Hitler's new weapons, the V1s and V2s, were creating havoc in London and the south-east of England. The V2 rockets were silent and deadly. They simply came out of the sky, landing indiscriminately with a horrendous explosion — to be *followed* by the approaching scream of the thing itself. The V1 "Buzz bomb" was every bit as effective, although our fighter planes did stand a reasonable chance of shooting down these pilotless planes before they reached London. When they *did* reach the capital, sometimes the engine stopped, the plane fell silently, hit a built-up area and caused devastation. Sometimes the engine stopped before the plane turned right round and glided in the opposite direction to reach another area unexpectedly. It was almost impossible for anyone on the ground to predict where and when the bombs would land.

But other things of interest to the soldiers were happening back home — signals of what might lie ahead for all of us when the war was over. The first prefabricated houses were being built for the returning heroes and their families. They were supposed to last ten years; I believe some of them still exist today! The government started the National Health Service and it also guaranteed education for everyone. These were the beginnings of the Welfare State which blossomed after the war. Another innovation — not so popular this time — was the start of a thing called "Pay As You Earn" which made every employer in Britain virtually a tax-collector for the government.

These were the items of news I tried to miniaturise

as snippets for our little newspaper. Frankly, all the time I was in France and Belgium I never heard of or saw one soldier gathering news from any other source at all. There were simply no newspapers or radio sets. The war was simply outside our hut doors — or at least a few miles away. "Anyway, who needs national or international news? Let's get it over and let's get home" — that was the cry.

There was *one* piece of news which I never reported in *The Craftsman*. It happened in our camp and the incident had such an effect on all of us in the Sergeants' Mess that Saturday night, I doubt if a report in my little newspaper would have been appreciated. Certainly I would not have been able to find the words to describe the situation.

I got back from Brussels to our camp near Ruisbroek. I was alone, and after I went through the camp gate I made for the Sergeants' Mess which was a large Nissen hut behind the tents.

Now, normally, the noise from our mess could be heard as far as the village, what with all the singing, shouting, drinking and talking. This night when I opened the door I could hear it squeaking on the hinges; you could have heard a pin being dropped.

Inside there was a crowd of Sergeants gathered in a semicircle listening to somebody in the middle who was talking in a low voice. Nobody moved; nobody made a sound. Everyone was listening, eyes staring and some mouths wide open. I tiptoed to the edge of the group, stood beside Sergeant Cooksley and looked at the speaker. It was Freddie Brown, a Staff-Sergeant who had been transferred four weeks previously from our base unit to a company on more active service "up front". I remembered that this six-foot, broad, tough, crewcut Cockney had pestered our CO for months for a posting to some frontline operation to "get a crack at 'em" before Germany collapsed. In desperation, the CO got him transferred to a small tank-recovery unit near the Rhine.

I put my mouth to Cooksley's ear. "What's he doing back here?"

He put his mouth to my ear. "Came back on three days' leave to see us."

"What's he telling them?"

"Listen."

It was then I saw Brown closely. He was sitting on a chair with a glass of beer in his hand and as he talked quietly I felt a shiver. He seemed to be almost weeping. He stopped, drank some beer and continued.

"Never drove a bulldozer before. My God — I soon learned. They just stuck me up on it an' said, 'You want a gas-mask?' but I said no, and we went at it. I reckon I shifted *tons* with that thing that day. 'Course I had to stop every half-hour or so an' vomit. Then I asked for the gas-mask." He stopped and took another swig of beer. "Arms an' legs an' half-bodies."

Somebody said quietly, "Into pits?"

He nodded. "Yeh — big pits. Then we filled them up. Well, I thought that was bad enough 'cos they were the dead ones. Then we saw those that were alive. That was worse. I'd often heard people talk about walkin' skeletons but this was the first time I'd ever seen them.

No kiddin' — they were just like skeletons covered over with skin an' they were crawlin' about wearin' these striped clothes. They couldn't even *talk* to us — even if I had known the lingo."

"How many of them?" somebody asked.

"Thousands of 'em, mate — bloody thousands. Hadn't eaten for ages an' ages. Diseased an' stinkin' an' . . ." He drank some more beer.

I had to know. I said, "Freddie — where *was* this?"

He looked up at me, red-eyed. "In Germany. After we crossed the Rhine. A place called Belsen."

"Who *were* these people?"

"I dunno. Some of them were from Poland and some Hungarians an' Czechoslovaks an' — most of them from the East."

"Prisoners of war?"

He shook his head.

"What, then?"

He shrugged. "I dunno. Just Jews that the Germans . . ." He stopped and wiped his eyes.

The group broke up in embarrassed silence and Freddie finished his beer.

We had just heard for the first time of a German extermination camp.

CHAPTER
TWENTY-ONE

Memories

Just the other day my wife said to me, "What did you feel about the abdication?"

"What abdication?"

She stared: "The Prince of Wales. Edward the Eighth."

"Not much."

"Not much! But that was in the 'thirties — and you were a teenager. Surely it had some effect on you."

I shrugged. "Maybe. I don't remember it as some shattering experience — not in *my* life, anyway. I suppose I was too busy playing my trumpet, doing my daily job, doing those showcards and posters for shops, writing little stories for magazines. I suppose I read about it in the papers, that's about all."

She sighed. "You must have had a funny set of priorities. In our family it was talked about for weeks."

Then I remembered something which I felt might improve her opinion of my priorities. "But I remember *meeting* the Prince of Wales."

"*Meeting* him? Where?"

"In Garrioch Road. He came to Glasgow on a tour and

the big line of motor cars came up from Queen Margaret Drive through Garrioch Road. Andy Russell and I were standing in the crowd just in front of the HLI Barracks. The Prince's car was leading the row and moving quite slow so that he could wave his hand to the crowds on either side. Andy and I ran out and ran alongside his car for quite a bit. His window was open and he smiled at me. I forget what I said but we were soon chased off by the police."

After this conversation which, may I say, did nothing to improve my status in my wife's eyes, I realised that most of our memories remain as images in our minds — like a photograph album. And we are selective, of course, remembering only the things which are to our credit, or at least those which don't bring a blush to our faces.

In the film *Citizen Kane*, the last word uttered by Orson Welles before he died was "Rosebud". Scores of reporters tried for a long time to discover why he uttered that word. Then at the end of the film it was made clear. "Rosebud" was the name of his little sledge from which he was parted when he was a boy.

It is those little snapshots of the mind's photo album which spark off memory. Pictures of various characters remain clear-cut and fresh while those of others — possibly more important people — are faded and blank simply because they made no impression on us.

One of the big scandals in Braeside Street I remember happened to the Weir family, and I always associated it somehow with the 12th of July, Orange Walk Day. Jimmy

200

Weir was a pal of mine whose mother was loud-mouthed and arrogant. Mr Weir was a fervent supporter of the Orange movement (I think he came originally from Northern Ireland). Every 12th of July he would appear in his navy-blue suit wearing an orange sash and a bowler hat. Then he would join the Grand Procession which assembled down at Hinshaw Street behind a flute band and he would step out, straight as a ramrod, with the other besashed and bowler-hatted enthusiasts up Maryhill Road while Jim and I watched them from the pavement. All this has nothing to do with Mr Weir's fall from grace, of course, but I always associate the Orange Walk with the fact that he ran off with a teenage girl in the factory where he was a foreman, never to return to the bellowing, outraged Mrs Weir. Somehow, I don't think his son Jim blamed him!

The Roman Catholic and Orange Protestant factions in Glasgow usually found expression for their conflict in the Rangers-Celtic football games. Indeed they still do. But now and then this emotional conflict bursts into flames on the Glasgow streets, and although we were never even singed in Maryhill by these conflagrations, elsewhere in the city some savage battles were fought — usually after a football match at Parkhead or at the home of the True Blues, Ibrox. I remember witnessing one of these fights from the top deck of a tramcar as we travelled through Bridgeton Cross. The fighting by young men with all sorts of weapons extended about three blocks, and the fire brigade were eventually called to turn the hoses on the crowds. Since our tramcar was stuck in the middle of this battle, I could witness the whole scene as if I was watching a civil war in progress.

Thankfully, nothing like this ever happened in Braeside Street. The only snapshot of violence I can remember was one which left me shocked for a long time. That was when a coal merchant's horse fell and broke its leg right in front of our close. I joined a group of children to see what would happen as the carter tried to get the animal back on its feet, then realised it was impossible. Then a man in a brown overall arrived, produced something like a gun, pointed it behind the horse's ear and there was a loud explosion. The horse kicked violently then lay still — dead.

More pleasant pictures come to my mind of the little scenes in that street. The Punch-and-Judy man, for instance. I can remember his face as if he were here now — sallow and with a large moustache. When he put the magic thing into his mouth he spoke in a squeaky voice and we were wide-eyed as he set up his stall — not in the back court like other street performers, but right out there in the front street at the top of the hill. Somehow he seemed to have a special dispensation for this site. And when he had finished the performance, the coppers wrapped in little bits of paper showered down on the pavement from the open windows above.

In a way, this "photo album" of the mind reveals clearer and more valid snapshots of one's early life than any bland black-and-white print. The sounds and smells of these little scenes come back . . . like the Co-operative Society grocery shop with its sawdust-covered floor and its carrier wires to take your cash directly to the cash kiosk then return with your receipt and — most importantly — your dividend evidence . . . or the wee home dairy at the bottom of the street, so typical of hundreds of those shops in the city which sold cooked meats and potted hough and scones baked on the premises . . . or the many pubs, one almost at every corner, right down Maryhill Road to St George's Cross; they had funny names like The Gushet Arms and the Tramcar Vaults (there was a model of a tramcar hung up outside) and Humphy MacFarlane's and others with Gaelic names which I couldn't pronounce (I expect these were so named to attract the Gaels).

Among the later pages in my "snapshot album" are some memories from those jazz days when I was playing my trumpet in small bands around the city. In the early 'thirties young people in Glasgow seemed to be dance-mad. There were small dance halls everywhere, and these were divided into two distinct groups — those that had ordinary ballroom dances like the foxtrot and the waltz and those which only provided "select" dancing, that is, formation dances like the "Embassy Tango" and the "Pride of Erin Waltz", the "Military Two-step" and other dances with queer-sounding names. The musicians in the small bands also fell into these two groups so that an ordinary jazz musician like me was usually out of his element in a "select" dance hall. He had to know the sequence thoroughly, and if he made a mistake, the Master of Ceremonies raised a row.

Saturday night was the busiest night for dance-hall musicians in the city. Also saxophone players and pianists and trumpet players were usually scarce simply because there weren't so many of them around. Thus, some bands to which I belonged had to settle for weird combinations on a Saturday in order to fulfil engagements.

I remember accepting an engagement to supply a five-piece band for a hall in Keith Street in Partick, and because the alto sax player could not turn up — he was ill — I had to settle for a one-string fiddle player. Yes, he actually produced his one-string job complete with a horn on the end. The rest of the band just stared while he "tuned" up. I must say this, though — his playing was superb. He didn't read a note but was always in key and took quite a few solos. The dance hall owner didn't complain and paid us out without a murmur — ten shillings each.

I remember one occasion when I was *not* paid for my performance. This was a small dance hall in Finnieston near the docks called Mick Brisbane's Hop. I should have seen the signs when we went into the place. There were only about a dozen dancers. And there were four of us.

We played all evening right through to ten-thirty. Then when the dancers had gone, Mr Brisbane himself — a short, squat man with a cherubic face and a nice smile held out his hands. "You see how it is, friends?"

"A poor night."

"Well, it's just as well it's only a small band you have to pay, isn't it?" said Dan Wheeler the pianist.

Mick smiled broadly and put his arm around my shoulders. "But I suppose that's the chance you fellows take when you do a gig. No dancers — no money."

Peter Hamilton the sax player lifted his head and said . . . quite loudly, "Now, just a minute!"

I touched his arm as I saw the two burly-looking men come out of Mick Brisbane's little room at the back of the hall. I said, "Peter — forget it."

"But I . . ."

"Forget it." I urged him and the other two towards the door.

Mr Brisbane was still smiling agreeably as we went out.

The first leave I got from the Orkney Islands deserved a photo-album of its own in terms of memory. It all started in Lyness on the island of Hoy. I joined hundreds of sailors, airmen and soldiers on the quay. The sea looked very rough and the sky was dark grey. I remember the name of the ship which was to take us across the Pentland Firth. It was the *Morialta*. The seas were so rough that day that the word came down through the crowd that the skipper was unwilling to set sail for Thurso. I don't know what happened; there was a commotion and I am sure that a few determined servicemen changed his mind, wild weather or not.

That trip was a nightmare. First we were taken out from Lyness in a ferryboat to the *Morialta* where we scrambled up rope ladders, fully-laden, to the heaving deck of the main ship. And this was us still in Scapa Flow, as one Corporal reminded us cheerfully. I was directed into the fo'castle where I sat between two sailors from the destroyer *Cossack*. When the *Morialta* set off through the Flow and past the cliffs of Hoy, the heaving was bad enough, but it was when we got into the Pentland Firth itself the ship almost stood on its stern.

There were times during that five-hour journey when I imagined I was in the Black Hole of Calcutta during the Indian riots. Somebody closed the steel door and those of us inside were left as if in a large elevator which rose and fell with sickening regularity. The operative word was "sickening". Every few minutes some serviceman would rush to that door, open it and be met with a great waterfall of sea water as it cascaded from the descending bows.

I sat quite rigid between those two old salts, grimly holding on to my dignity and my stomach contents. Then the sailor on my right said, "Feelin' a bit dicky, son, are ye?"

I said nothing as I felt the tightness around my throat.

He continued, "I'll tell you what we do aboard the *Cossack* with young sailors on their first voyage. We tie a lump of pig-fat on to a piece of string and we lower that down his throat . . ."

"Excuse me." I jumped up and made for the door, waterfall or no waterfall. When I got out on the howling, swirling sea-soaked deck I clung to a mast and as I seemed to bring my boots up, I heard the 3-inch gun on the bow firing. I paid no attention. The ship could have been torpedoed for all I cared. I learned later that we were firing at what could have been a mine.

There are possibly hundreds more of these little snapshot pictures in my life-album as, no doubt, there are in most people's memory. The watershed for all of us at my age was that war. We went into it by accident or design to play one role or another, some with distinction, some with none. I belonged to the latter category.

Like most of my contemporaries from little streets like Braeside Street in one Maryhill or another in one city or another, I went in as a boy and came out almost seven years later all the man I could ever hope to be.

Certainly, for good or bad, we were never the same people again. The old attitudes changed over these years and were replaced by new ideas of wealth-sharing and a truly classless society. Whether these ideals were ever achieved — or ever *could* be achieved — whether it became a land fit for heroes and heroines, is open to question, depending on where you stand. Socialism and the Welfare State were the order of the day. Poverty and mass unemployment and means tests and slums were to be banished forever. Nobody would touch their forelock to anyone any more. A new day had come to Britain.

For my part, the road from that one-room house in Braeside Street has been a pleasant one; perhaps not strewn with roses all the way, but certainly filled with variety, and my companions along that way have, in the main, been the salt of the earth. But my father's socialist Valhalla never happened.

ISIS publish a wide range of books in large print, from fiction to biography. A full list of titles is available free of charge from the address below. Alternatively, contact your local library for details of their collection of ISIS large print books.

Details of ISIS complete and unabridged audio books are also available.

Any suggestions for books you would like to see in large print or audio are always welcome.

7 Centremead
Osney Mead
Oxford OX2 0ES
(01865) 250333

ISIS REMINISCENCE SERIES

The ISIS Reminiscence Series has been developed with the older reader in mind. Well-loved in their own right, these titles have been chosen for their memory-evoking content.

FRED ARCHER
The Cuckoo Pen
The Distant Scene
The Village Doctor

BRENDA BULLOCK
A Pocket With A Hole

WILLIAM COOPER
From Early Life

KATHLEEN DAYUS
All My Days
The Best of Times
Her People

DENIS FARRIER
Country Vet

WINIFRED FOLEY
Back to the Forest
No Pipe Dreams for Father

PEGGY GRAYSON
Buttercup Jill

JACK HARGREAVES
The Old Country

ISIS REMINISCENCE SERIES

ISIS REMINISCENCE SERIES

SHEILA STEWART
Lifting the Latch

JEAN STONE & LOUISE BRODIE
Tales of the Old Gardeners

EDWARD STOREY
In Fen Country Heaven
Fen Boy First

NANCY THOMPSON
At Their Departing

MARRIE WALSH
An Irish Country Childhood

RODERICK WILKINSON
Memories of Maryhill

BIOGRAPHY & AUTOBIOGRAPHY

NINA BAWDEN
In My Own Time

SALLY BECKER
The Angel of Mostar

CHRISTABEL BIELENBERG
The Road Ahead

CAROLINE BLACKWOOD
The Last of the Duchess

ALAN BLOOM
Come You Here, Boy!

ADRIENNE BLUE
Martina Unauthorized

BARBARA CARTLAND
I Reach for the Stars

CATRINE CLAY
Princess to Queen

JILL KERR CONWAY
True North

DAVID DAY
The Bevin Boy

MARGARET DURRELL
Whatever Happened to Margo?

BIOGRAPHY & AUTOBIOGRAPHY

MONICA EDWARDS
The Unsought Farm
The Cats of Punchbowl Farm

CHRISTOPHER FALKUS
The Life and Times of Charles II

LADY FORTESCUE
Sunset House

EUGENIE FRASER
The Dvina Remains
The House By the Dvina

KIT FRASER
Toff Down Pit

KENNETH HARRIS
The Queen

DON HAWORTH
The Fred Dibnah Story

PAUL HEINEY
Pulling Punches
Second Crop

SARA HENDERSON
From Strength to Strength

PAUL JAMES
Princess Alexandra

BIOGRAPHY & AUTOBIOGRAPHY

EILEEN JONES
Neil Kinnock

JAMES LEITH
Ironing John

FLAVIA LENG
Daphne du Maurier

MARGARET LEWIS
Edith Pargeter: Ellis Peters

VICTORIA MASSEY
One Child's War

NORMAN MURSELL
Come Dawn, Come Dusk

MICHAEL NICHOLSON
Natasha's Story

LESLEY O'BRIEN
Mary MacKillop Unveiled

ADRIAN PLASS
The Sacred Diary of Adrian Plass Aged 37 ³/₄

CHRIS RYAN
The One That Got Away

J. OSWALD SANDERS
Enjoying Your Best Years

VERNON SCANNELL
Drums of Morning

BIOGRAPHY & AUTOBIOGRAPHY

STEPHANIE SLATER WITH PAT LANCASTER
Beyond Fear

DAVA SOBEL
Longitude

DOUGLAS SUTHERLAND
Against the Wind
Born Yesterday

ALICE TAYLOR
The Night Before Christmas

SOPHIE THURNHAM
Sophie's Journey

CHRISTOPHER WILSON
A Greater Love

GENERAL NON-FICTION

RICHARD, EARL OF BRADFORD
Stately Secrets

WILLIAM CASH
Educating William

CLIVE DUNN
Permission to Laugh

EMMA FORD
Countrywomen

LADY FORTESCUE
Sunset House

JOANNA GOLDSWORTHY
Mothers: Reflections by Daughters

PATRICIA GREEN, CHARLES COLLINGWOOD
& HEIDI NIKLAUS
The Book of The Archers

HELENE HANFF
Letter From New York

ANDREW & MARIA HUBERT
A Wartime Christmas

MARGARET HUMPHREYS
Empty Cradles

JAMES LEITH
Ironing John

LESLEY LEWIS
The Private Life Of A Country House